Generative AI for Web Development

Building Web Applications Powered by OpenAI APIs and Next.js

Tom Auger
Emma Saroyan

Apress®

Generative AI for Web Development: Building Web Applications Powered by OpenAI APIs and Next.js

Tom Auger
Edinburgh, Midlothian, UK

Emma Saroyan
Yerevan, Armenia

ISBN-13 (pbk): 979-8-8688-0884-5
https://doi.org/10.1007/979-8-8688-0885-2

ISBN-13 (electronic): 979-8-8688-0885-2

Copyright © 2024 by Tom Auger and Emma Saroyan

This work is subject to copyright. All rights are reserved by the Publisher, whether the whole or part of the material is concerned, specifically the rights of translation, reprinting, reuse of illustrations, recitation, broadcasting, reproduction on microfilms or in any other physical way, and transmission or information storage and retrieval, electronic adaptation, computer software, or by similar or dissimilar methodology now known or hereafter developed.

Trademarked names, logos, and images may appear in this book. Rather than use a trademark symbol with every occurrence of a trademarked name, logo, or image we use the names, logos, and images only in an editorial fashion and to the benefit of the trademark owner, with no intention of infringement of the trademark.

The use in this publication of trade names, trademarks, service marks, and similar terms, even if they are not identified as such, is not to be taken as an expression of opinion as to whether or not they are subject to proprietary rights.

While the advice and information in this book are believed to be true and accurate at the date of publication, neither the authors nor the editors nor the publisher can accept any legal responsibility for any errors or omissions that may be made. The publisher makes no warranty, express or implied, with respect to the material contained herein.

Managing Director, Apress Media LLC: Welmoed Spahr
Acquisitions Editor: James Robinson-Prior
Desk Editor: James Markham
Editorial Project Manager: Gryffin Winkler

Cover designed by eStudioCalamar

Cover Image by Gerd Altmann from Pixabay

Distributed to the book trade worldwide by Springer Science+Business Media New York, 1 New York Plaza, Suite 4600, New York, NY 10004-1562, USA. Phone 1-800-SPRINGER, fax (201) 348-4505, e-mail orders-ny@springer-sbm.com, or visit www.springeronline.com. Apress Media, LLC is a California LLC and the sole member (owner) is Springer Science + Business Media Finance Inc (SSBM Finance Inc). SSBM Finance Inc is a **Delaware** corporation.

For information on translations, please e-mail booktranslations@springernature.com; for reprint, paperback, or audio rights, please e-mail bookpermissions@springernature.com.

Apress titles may be purchased in bulk for academic, corporate, or promotional use. eBook versions and licenses are also available for most titles. For more information, reference our Print and eBook Bulk Sales web page at http://www.apress.com/bulk-sales.

Any source code or other supplementary material referenced by the author in this book is available to readers on GitHub. For more detailed information, please visit https://www.apress.com/gp/services/source-code.

If disposing of this product, please recycle the paper

Մեր սիրելի ծնողներին՝ մեզ միշտ հավատալու համար:

To our dear parents, who always believed in us.

Table of Contents

About the Authors xi

About the Technical Reviewer xiii

Acknowledgments xv

Introduction xvii

Part I: Generative AI 1

Chapter 1: What Is Generative AI? 3
1.1 Introduction 3
1.2 In the Beginning 4
1.3 The Research Transforming AI 6
1.4 The Birth of ChatGPT 7
1.5 Imagining New Worlds 10
1.6 Web Development in the AI Era 12
1.7 Summary 13

Chapter 2: Legal, Ethical, and Security Considerations 15
2.1 Introduction 15
2.2 Copyright and Liability 15
2.3 Veracity and Deepfakes 17
2.4 Bias and Fairness 21
2.5 Security and Safety 23
2.6 Summary 25

TABLE OF CONTENTS

Chapter 3: Introduction to ChatGPT 27
3.1 Introduction 27
3.2 What Is ChatGPT? 27
3.3 Hello ChatGPT 29
3.3.1 Prompting with Chains of Thought 34
3.3.2 Multimodal Prompting 36
3.4 How Does ChatGPT Work? 38
3.4.1 Tokenization and Text Prediction 39
3.4.2 System Prompt and Custom Instructions 43
3.5 Summary 46

Chapter 4: Introduction to DALL-E 47
4.1 Introduction 47
4.2 What Is DALL-E? 47
4.3 Generating Images with DALL-E 3 49
4.4 Edits and Variations of Images 56
4.5 Summary 62

Chapter 5: Building Web Apps with ChatGPT and DALL-E 63
5.1 Introduction 63
5.2 Setting Up the Project 63
5.2.1 Installing Prerequisites 64
5.2.2 Creating the Next.js App 65
5.2.3 Cleaning the Project Template 68
5.3 Building the Home Page 69
5.4 Building the Product Pages 79
5.5 Building the Contact Page 83
5.6 Summary 84

TABLE OF CONTENTS

Chapter 6: Overview of the OpenAI APIs 87

6.1 Introduction 87

6.2 What Are the OpenAI APIs? 87

6.3 Pricing and Usage 88

    6.3.1 Chat API Pricing 89

    6.3.2 Image API Pricing 90

    6.3.3 Pricing of Other OpenAI APIs 91

    6.3.4 Batch Pricing 91

    6.3.5 Pay-As-You-Go with Credits 92

    6.3.6 Usage Limits 92

6.4 Creating an API Account and API Key 94

    6.4.1 Creating an API Account 95

    6.4.2 Creating an API Key 98

    6.4.3 Keeping Your API Key Secure 100

6.5 Experimenting with the API Playground 102

    6.5.1 Adjusting Parameters 104

6.6 Using the OpenAI APIs with Next.js 107

    6.6.1 Setting Up the Next.js Project 107

    6.6.2 Generating the UI 108

    6.6.3 Adding an OpenAI API Key 110

    6.6.4 Generating Content with the OpenAI APIs 111

6.7 Summary 116

Chapter 7: Alternative Models to OpenAI 117

7.1 Introduction 117

7.2 Alternative Text Generation Models 117

    7.2.1 Google Gemini 118

    7.2.2 Anthropic Claude 120

TABLE OF CONTENTS

- 7.2.3 Meta LLama 121
- 7.2.4 Mistral 122
- 7.3 Alternative Image Generation Models 123
  - 7.3.1 Stable Diffusion 123
  - 7.3.2 Midjourney 126
- 7.4 Summary 128

Part II: Building Generative AI–Powered Web Apps 131

Chapter 8: Building a Story/Poetry Generator 133

- 8.1 Introduction 133
- 8.2 Setting Up the Project 133
  - 8.2.1 Configuring an OpenAI API Key 135
- 8.3 Creating the UI 136
- 8.4 Creating the Backend 141
  - 8.4.1 Generating the Story 141
- 8.5 Generating Different Types of Literature 146
  - 8.5.1 Generating Different Genres 146
  - 8.5.2 Generating Poetry 149
- 8.6 Generating Illustrations 151
- 8.7 Adding a Library Page 156
  - 8.7.1 Saving the Stories 156
  - 8.7.2 Building the Library UI 159
- 8.8 Creating a Home Page 162
- 8.9 Summary 164

Chapter 9: Building a Language Learning App 165

- 9.1 Introduction 165
- 9.2 Setting Up the Project 166
  - 9.2.1 Configuring an OpenAI API Key 167

TABLE OF CONTENTS

9.3 Creating a Vocabulary Translating Quiz 168
    9.3.1 Building the Backend 168
    9.3.2 Implementing the UI 175

9.4 Creating a Vocabulary Spelling Quiz 182
    9.4.1 Building the Backend 182
    9.4.2 Implementing the UI 187

9.5 Creating a Home Page 193

9.6 Summary 195

Chapter 10: Building a Blog with a Custom Chatbot 197

10.1 Introduction 197

10.2 Setting Up the Project 198
    10.2.1 Configuring an OpenAI API Key 199

10.3 Creating a Basic Blog 200
    10.3.1 Creating the Blog Skeleton 200
    10.3.2 Adding Content 204
    10.3.3 Adding Styles 206

10.4 Creating an Assistant 207
    10.4.1 Fine-Tuning and RAG 208
    10.4.2 Building and Testing an Assistant 210

10.5 Adding a Chat Interface 216
    10.5.1 Building the Backend 216
    10.5.2 Building the UI 222
    10.5.3 Adding a Pop-Up Chat 227

10.6 Summary 228

Chapter 11: The Future of Generative AI 231

11.1 Introduction 231

11.2 The Future of Generative AI 231

TABLE OF CONTENTS

    11.2.1 Open Source vs. Closed Source 232
    11.2.2 Generalist vs. Specialized LLMs 235
    11.2.3 Regulated vs. Unregulated 236
    11.2.4 Transformers vs. Another Architecture 237
  11.3 Further Reading 238
  11.4 Summary 239

Index 241

About the Authors

Tom Auger is a senior software engineer with extensive experience in building web APIs and web applications for both startups and large enterprises. As an increasing number of breakthroughs were made in AI, Tom decided to take a sabbatical and obtained a master's degree in Computer Science at Edinburgh University researching AI, machine learning, and computer security in greater depth. Tom regularly teaches workshops and bootcamps on generative AI. He currently leads the development of AI in education at the TUMO Center for Creative Technologies to build an AI-powered learning coach.

Emma Saroyan graduated with a BS in Computer Science from the American University of Armenia and is currently a developer advocate with a focus on developer products, platforms, and APIs. Before that, she worked at startups at the intersection of technology and education. Emma regularly speaks at international open source conferences and is an active advocate for women in tech serving on the DISC Committee of NumFOCUS, an organization dedicated to supporting and advancing open source scientific computing projects. She believes we are at one of the biggest inflection points in human history, given the disruption that generative AI is creating.

About the Technical Reviewer

Astha Puri is an accomplished data scientist specializing in responsible AI practices, with a significant focus on healthcare. Currently, she is serving as a Senior Data Scientist at a Fortune 10 company in New York. Astha has a demonstrated history of architecting innovative AI-driven solutions that enhance user experiences, optimize operations, and uphold ethical standards in tech companies like Oracle and Twilio and now is bringing that expertise to the healthcare domain. Her expertise lies in designing and implementing advanced machine learning models, particularly in recommendation systems, natural language processing, and real-time data processing.

Astha holds a master's degree in Business Analytics from the University of Minnesota's Carlson School of Management and a B.Tech. in Electronics and Communication Engineering from VIT University. She has further honed her skills with an Executive Certificate in Machine Learning in Business from MIT.

Throughout her career, Astha has consistently applied her technical acumen to address complex challenges, earning recognition through numerous award nominations such as the Excellence in Applied Research Award and the Health 2.0 Excellence in Healthcare Award. She has also been named one of the Top 250 Remarkable Women in AI and ML. Her contributions extend beyond her professional work, as she actively participates in book reviews, journal publications, and open source

ABOUT THE TECHNICAL REVIEWER

projects. She is part of the core national team and AI lead in the Indian Fertility Society developing their AI solutions. Astha is also an ambassador for Google's Women Techmakers and WiDS (Women in Data Science) at Stanford University. She is the founding board member and VP of her nonprofit W2D2 (Women Who Do Data) reflecting her commitment to empowering future AI professionals and promoting gender equity in tech.

Acknowledgments

Writing a book on generative AI, a technology that is changing the world at an unprecedented pace, is a unique challenge and one that could not have been achieved alone. We are deeply grateful to our editor, James Robinson-Prior, for giving us the opportunity to write this book and for his support and patience throughout. Our thanks also go to our technical reviewer, Astha Puri, whose feedback and suggestions have improved the quality of this work. We are equally grateful to Shobana Srinivasan for keeping us on track and ensuring the timely completion of this book. Our appreciation extends to the entire team at Apress, whose efforts were essential in bringing this book to fruition. Lastly, and most importantly, we wish to thank our families for their unwavering support and love during this journey.

Introduction

When ChatGPT was released in November 2022, it caught the world by surprise. Since 2012, artificial intelligence had already gone through a renaissance, beginning with the release of AlexNet, an image recognition model, that outperformed the state of the art by over 10% – a significant margin. However, progress in the following years was slow. At that time, building competitive AI systems required talented engineers, large amounts of data, and an equally large financial budget, putting it out of reach of all but large companies and well-funded startups. By 2021, enthusiasm for AI was starting to dwindle as the pace of progress slowed.

The most radical move by OpenAI with ChatGPT wasn't simply building the technology itself, which was already impressive, but the decision to release it to the whole world free of charge. For the first time, a state-of-the-art AI system was available to everyone with an Internet connection to experiment with. One of the first industries to recognize the utility of generative AI was software engineering. ChatGPT was not only able to write prose but also program code. Engineers, instead of going to sites like Stack Overflow to find answers to questions, began asking them to ChatGPT and getting the solutions directly.

Since 2022, ChatGPT has become more advanced, and rival companies are competing to build the most intelligent chatbot. Generative AI is now being embedded across a wide range of applications, enhancing features and capabilities. As a result, software engineers are increasingly engaging with generative AI, both as a tool to boost their productivity in coding and as a feature to integrate into their companies' systems.

This book is aimed at web developers who are new to generative AI and want to learn how to use it effectively. Part 1 of this book gives an overview of generative AI. In Chapter 1, we begin with a quick tour through

INTRODUCTION

the history of generative AI, from its inception in the 1970s to the current day. In Chapter 2, we then review the legal, ethical, and security challenges that generative AI presents to allow you to understand the risks of using it. In Chapters 3 and 4, we introduce OpenAI's flagship products: ChatGPT for text generation and DALL-E for image generation. In Chapter 5, we explore how to use ChatGPT and DALL-E to generate a simple web application, with examples and strategies for writing prompts. In Chapter 6, we introduce the OpenAI APIs and explore how to integrate generative AI functionality into web applications. Chapter 7 concludes this part of the book with a review of rival generative AI tools from companies competing with OpenAI.

In Part 2 of this book, we put all the knowledge together to build three example web applications with Next.js, incorporating features powered by generative AI using the OpenAI APIs. We use ChatGPT to assist with generating the code, showing how to write effective prompts to build applications rapidly. In Chapter 8, we build a story and poetry generator using GPT-4o to generate the story text and DALL-E to generate illustrations. In Chapter 9, we build a language learning app showcasing how to generate structured outputs with GPT-4o and build dynamic web applications. In Chapter 10, we build a blog with a chatbot widget customized on the blog posts to enable users to ask questions and converse with them. Finally in Chapter 11, we conclude the book with a look to the future and predict how generative AI will evolve next.

The chapters of this book are self-contained and can be read in any order. If you are already familiar with ChatGPT and DALL-E, you may wish to skip to Chapter 6 to learn about the OpenAI APIs and how they work. If you are looking to get hands-on immediately, start with Chapter 8 to begin building a story and poetry generator step by step.

Finally, thank you for choosing to read this book. Learning how to use generative AI effectively is the most important skill every web developer should learn today. We hope you enjoy reading this book and that it helps you on your journey to mastering AI-driven web development.

PART I

Generative AI

CHAPTER 1

What Is Generative AI?

1.1 Introduction

Generative artificial intelligence (AI) is a transformative technology that is rapidly reshaping the world. What was once a far-off dream – a machine capable of human-like communication and reasoning – is fast becoming a reality. Staying current in the tech industry requires mastering the latest innovations. This book is designed for web developers, from novices to experts, providing an introduction to generative AI and practical guidance on integrating it into web applications.

The first part of this book explores generative AI, outlining its capabilities and limitations, and introduces the leading tools and APIs from OpenAI: ChatGPT and DALL-E. The second part offers a practical guide, where we will build web applications using Next.js, demonstrating how generative AI can bring intelligence to your projects and enhance your productivity as a developer.

In order to understand what generative AI is and what it is capable of, it is necessary to understand the history of its development. In this chapter, we tell the story of generative AI from its inception to the present day and explain why this is the most important technology for web developers to learn today.

CHAPTER 1   WHAT IS GENERATIVE AI?

1.2 In the Beginning

Since the artificial intelligence (AI) boom began in the early 2010s, experts have speculated on the next major AI breakthrough and its global impact. Early on, one of the most active research areas was object detection: the task of identifying and listing all objects in a photo, whether animals, pencils, or other items. In 2012, three academic researchers – Alex Krizhevsky, Ilya Sutskever, and Geoffrey Hinton – published a paper introducing AlexNet,[1] an AI trained on over one million images. It could identify objects from a list of 1,000 possibilities with remarkable accuracy. What truly captured the attention of the research community was AlexNet's performance in the 2012 ImageNet Visual Recognition Challenge, where it achieved a top 5 error rate that was 10.3% lower than the second-best competitor – a significant leap forward.

The progress AlexNet had made in object detection sparked a tsunami of investment in AI. Now that computers could "see" the world around them, cars could become fully autonomous, medical imaging devices could diagnose abnormalities, and security cameras could alert law enforcement to active crimes. But despite all the promise and hype, AI technology was still too primitive to deliver on these dreams. Security researchers developed "adversarial attacks" by placing specially crafted stickers on traffic stop signs so the AI interpreted them as 60 MPH speed limits. The accuracy rate for detecting medical abnormalities never reached levels to compete with human radiographers, and the introduction of data privacy laws such as GDPR in Europe and the United States effectively outlawed using AI for automatic crime detection.

---

[1] AlexNet paper: https://proceedings.neurips.cc/paper_files/paper/2012/file/c399862d3b9d6b76c8436e924a68c45b-Paper.pdf

But while the spotlight was on using AI for detection and prediction, a significant parallel development was quietly unfolding. In 2014, researcher Ian Goodfellow was searching for methods to enhance AI performance and developed the following novel idea. Traditionally, AI training relies on providing a list of samples along with the expected outputs – the more samples, the better the performance. But what if you don't have many samples, perhaps because the data is rare or hard to obtain? The trick Goodfellow developed is to train two AIs: one that generates sample data and another that makes predictions based on that data. The training process pits these two AIs against each other, where one is trying to generate good training data and the other validates whether the generated data are realistic. Goodfellow called such a system a "generative adversarial network" or GAN, and it worked, with impressive results. Not only did this approach produce superior predictor models, it also created impressive generator models, particularly for generating images.

One intriguing application of GANs is the creation of fake human portraits. In 2018, a team of researchers at Nvidia developed StyleGAN which creates human faces so realistic that Uber engineer Phillip Wang built the website (`https://thispersondoesnotexist.com/`) which uses the software to generate and display a new portrait on every page reload (see Figure 1-1 for an example). While these developments were entertaining, if not disconcerting, there weren't many practical use cases for them. The problem is that each GAN can only be trained for a specific type of image generation: a GAN designed to create human faces cannot also generate images of cats. Since training AIs is expensive and time-consuming, this makes it impractical to use GANs beyond niche applications. It would take another major breakthrough in AI research to achieve the kind of generative AI we see today.

CHAPTER 1   WHAT IS GENERATIVE AI?

Figure 1-1. *This person does not exist! A fake image of a girl generated with StyleGAN*[2]

1.3 The Research Transforming AI

In 2017, a team of researchers at Google Brain published a groundbreaking paper[3] titled "Attention Is All You Need" describing a new method for training AIs to generate content. This approach, known as the *transformer architecture*, revolutionizes how an AI interprets and trains on data, especially data that comes in sequences, like words and sentences in text. Unlike GANs, the transformer architecture enables an AI to analyze input samples in order and discern the relationships between them with greater sophistication. The result is an AI with a deeper understanding of data relationships and their most probable orderings.

The challenge of generating content where the order of the output matters is at the heart of AIs that produce natural language, where words and sentences must appear in a coherent order. These AIs, called large language

---

[2] Generated by https://thispersondoesnotexist.com/
[3] "Attention Is All You Need" paper: https://arxiv.org/abs/1706.03762

models (LLMs), are trained on a vast corpus of text, taken from books and web pages across the Internet. However, the transformer architecture is complex and demands significant computational power. Scaling this approach to train an AI on large text datasets requires considerable financial and technical resources. But one startup, called OpenAI, had the financing and some of the best technical and theoretical expertise to tackle this challenge. In 2018, OpenAI released their first LLM built with the transformer architecture, known as the generative pretrained transformer, or GPT. While it outperformed existing LLMs, it was only effective at completing partial sentences and short passages, and due to the limited size of its training corpus, its knowledge was limited to a narrow range of topics.

OpenAI continued to scale their GPT technology, releasing GPT-2 in February 2019. At over 12 times the size of the first iteration, GPT-2 was able to generate longer coherent passages and, with more data in its training corpus, could produce content on a wider variety of topics. However, there were still many limitations where the AI would frequently produce nonsensical output. OpenAI then scaled their technology once more, again by 12 times, and in June 2020 released GPT-3. It was at this point that OpenAI's researchers discovered something remarkable – the outputs produced by this AI were extremely good. Almost *humanly* good. But while this AI was made available for anyone to use, it wasn't simple to interact with. The only way to communicate with GPT-3 was to give it some words or sentences and then get it to generate a continuation of the text. Fortunately, OpenAI had ideas to make it easier for humans to interact with its GPT technology, and after 18 months of development, it released a tool that kick-started the next revolution in AI.

1.4 The Birth of ChatGPT

In November 2022, OpenAI released a chatbot powered by their GPT-3 technology called ChatGPT. It was quick to respond, had a memory of

CHAPTER 1   WHAT IS GENERATIVE AI?

the conversation, and had knowledge of a wide range of topics. But the most remarkable thing was that OpenAI provided access free of charge to everyone on the planet. Just two months after its release, ChatGPT had over 100 million active users, making it one of the fastest growing applications in history, beaten only by Threads which capitalized on its existing user base from Facebook and Instagram (Figure 1-2). And this was just the beginning. In March 2023, the fourth iteration of the GPT technology, GPT-4, was released and integrated into ChatGPT. The family of GPT-4 models are, at the time of writing, the most powerful and sophisticated LLMs ever created, and as we will explore in this book, they are capable of generating remarkably human-like content.

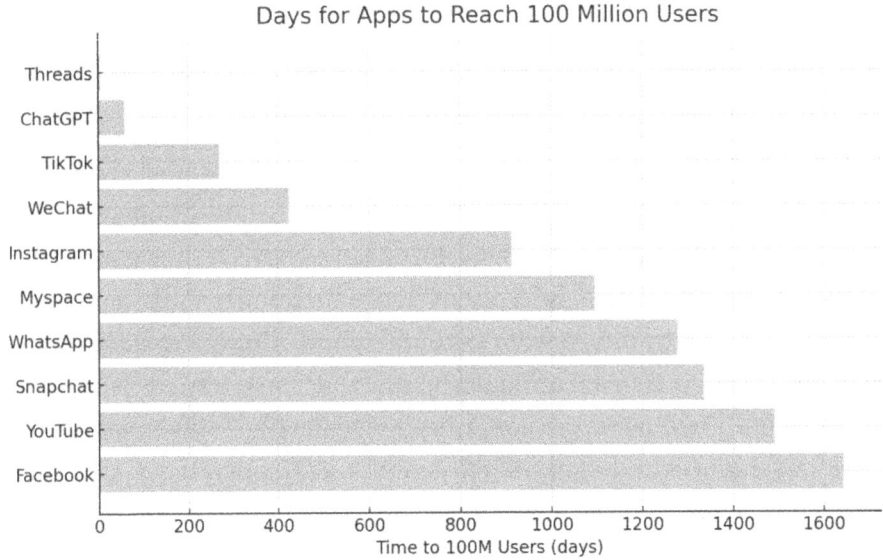

Figure 1-2. Number of days for apps to reach 100 million users[4]

---

[4] Data source: https://www.visualcapitalist.com/threads-100-million-users/

CHAPTER 1   WHAT IS GENERATIVE AI?

Since the release of ChatGPT, OpenAI has continued to add features and improvements to the interface, which we will introduce and explore in more detail in Chapter 3. The key question every tech pundit is asking now is: what will come next? OpenAI has clearly stated their goal – to create an artificial general intelligence (AGI), an AI with intelligence equal or superior to humans. While the progress over the last two years is impressive and given the substantial quantities of investment and intellectual energy focused on AI, there will certainly be more advances, it is premature to make any predictions about the advent of AGI. The more pressing question is what the impact of current AI technology, and its upcoming advances, will be on the world.

The impressive performance and commercial success of ChatGPT is predicted to have a big impact on employee productivity, especially in customer service, marketing, and software engineering. A 2022 report by McKinsey[5] predicts that generative AI could increase labor productivity across the global economy by 0.1–0.6 percent annually. The fields of software engineering and web development in particular are heavily impacted by ChatGPT. Its ability to generate code and provide technical advice competes with the performance of human engineers. Although ChatGPT has many limitations, which we will examine in detail in Chapter 2, the widespread adoption of this tool by developers indicates that it is rapidly becoming an essential tool in the industry.

While ChatGPT has been revolutionizing text generation, the same transformer technology is being applied to produce other types of content including images, video, and music, with equally spectacular results.

---

[5] "The economic potential of generative AI: The next productivity frontier," McKinsey: https://www.mckinsey.com/capabilities/mckinsey-digital/our-insights/the-economic-potential-of-generative-AI-the-next-productivity-frontier#introduction

1.5 Imagining New Worlds

While ChatGPT transformed chatbots, the same transformer architecture that powered it was also being applied to generate images. In January 2021, OpenAI released DALL-E, the name being a portmanteau of the artist Salvador Dalí and the Pixar character WALL-E, which generates images from a text description. The initial version, while functional, was relatively primitive, only capable of interpreting basic objects and styles from the given prompt. However, rapid advancements followed, with DALL-E 2 released in April 2022 and DALL-E 3 in October 2023. The latest version is capable of generating photorealistic images with remarkable levels of detail and employs ChatGPT behind the scenes to write detailed prompts to aid the generation process. Buoyed by the success of OpenAI, rival companies have been training generative image AIs too, the most notable being Midjourney, capable of generating hyperrealistic images in a wide range of artistic styles such as the example in Figure 1-3. DALL-E will be explored in greater detail in Chapter 4.

CHAPTER 1   WHAT IS GENERATIVE AI?

Figure 1-3. *A futuristic impression of the city of Yerevan, Armenia, generated by Midjourney*[6]

The power of these image-generating AIs is as impressive as it is controversial. The quality of the content rivals that of professional artists, raising concerns about the potential economic impact on creative industries. Ultimately, it is our choice as consumers whether we value and appreciate art produced by humans over that produced by machines. From an economic perspective, the market will likely dictate the price we're willing to pay for art, based on supply and demand. If machines can now produce art of comparable quality at a lower cost, then this is the new economic reality artists must contend with. The ethical, legal, and security implications of generative AI will be explored in more detail in Chapter 2.

---

[6] Midjourney: https://www.midjourney.com/

1.6 Web Development in the AI Era

One of the fields most affected by generative AI is software engineering. A long-standing meme in the developer community jokes that the job is largely copy and pasting existing code from the Internet. While this may have been an exaggeration in the past, it's becoming a reality today, as developers increasingly rely on AI tools like ChatGPT and GitHub Copilot to generate code more quickly and efficiently than they could on their own. Developers are also using ChatGPT to debug and explain code, making it clear that these AI tools are becoming indispensable assets in every software engineer's toolkit.

In web development, where engineers often work across a broad technical stack from backend to frontend, AI code assistants like ChatGPT offer significant productivity gains. A key aspect of a software engineer's role is continuous learning and staying on top of technological trends. Just as knowing how to write clean code and create good tests distinguishes great engineers from good ones, the effective use of AI tools will become the defining skill that sets the most productive engineers apart from the rest.

The goal of this book is to showcase the latest techniques and best practices for using generative AI in web development through practical examples. By focusing on hands-on applications, you can immediately implement these concepts in your own projects. However, AI is evolving rapidly, and by the time you read this book, there may already be new features and versions of the tools discussed. Generative AI is an experimental field; what matters is the approach and core techniques which will remain relevant and applicable for the foreseeable future. These are the most valuable and pertinent insights that you will gain as we explore this fascinating and exciting topic.

1.7 Summary

In this chapter, we introduced the following:

- The technical breakthroughs in the history of the development of generative AI from GANs to GPTs.

- OpenAI's generative AI tools including ChatGPT and DALL-E.

- The impact of generative AI in web development and how it can improve developer productivity.

In Chapter 2, we will introduce and discuss in detail the legal, ethical, and security considerations of using generative AI.

CHAPTER 2

Legal, Ethical, and Security Considerations

2.1 Introduction

While generative AI promises significant benefits to our personal and professional lives, it also presents certain risks. In this chapter, we examine the legal, ethical, and security concerns that should be considered before adopting generative AI. This discussion is not comprehensive, nor should it be taken as legal advice. The aim is to highlight key issues, enabling you to assess whether generative AI is suitable for your project and whether the associated risks are acceptable.

2.2 Copyright and Liability

Generative AI is capable of producing high-quality output that can be copied and used immediately. However, it is crucial to verify whether this is allowed under the terms of the AI service you are using. For

CHAPTER 2   LEGAL, ETHICAL, AND SECURITY CONSIDERATIONS

example, according to OpenAI's Terms of Use[1] as of February 2024, full ownership is granted to both the inputs you provide and the outputs generated:

> *Ownership of Content. As between you and OpenAI, and to the extent permitted by applicable law, you (a) retain your ownership rights in Input and (b) own the Output. We hereby assign to you all our right, title, and interest, if any, in and to Output.*

If you are using an AI system from another provider, it is important to review the ownership and usage rights before using the outputs for anything beyond personal use.

While the terms grant full ownership of generated content, it does not mean that the content is entirely original. Generative AI is trained on vast datasets, and while many are open source or publicly available, not all of them are free from copyright restrictions. As a result, generative AI may inadvertently produce outputs that closely resemble existing copyrighted material, potentially leading to infringement claims. Additionally, the generated content may not be unique, as OpenAI cautions in their terms:

> *Output may not be unique and other users may receive similar output from our Services*

The responsibility typically lies with users and developers to ensure that the generated content does not violate copyright laws. If you plan to use generative AI content for anything beyond personal use, particularly for commercial purposes, it is advisable to seek legal advice first.

---

[1] https://openai.com/policies/terms-of-use/

2.3 Veracity and Deepfakes

The randomness inherent in generative AI is a double-edged sword. On the one hand, it induces creativity resulting in novel outputs, but on the other, it can cause "hallucinations" where the AI produces information that appears to be true, sometimes convincingly so, but actually is fiction. Generative AIs lack an intrinsic understanding of what is true and false and have limited capabilities to follow logic, making them susceptible to generating outputs with flawed reasoning and contradictions. In one case, researchers found that if ChatGPT was given the statement "A is B" in its training set, it would correctly assert when prompted that "A is B," but when asked if "B is A," it would state this was false.[2] For example, when the LLM was trained on the sentence "Valentina Tereshkova was the first woman to travel to space," it failed to correctly answer the question "Who was the first woman to travel to space?" – instead replying with a different name or claiming not to know the answer. An entertaining demonstration of ChatGPT's inability to reason is to prompt it to solve simple logic puzzles, to which it provides absurdly complex solutions such as in Figure 2-1.

---

[2] "The Reversal Curse: LLMs trained on "A is B" fail to learn "B is A"" – https://arxiv.org/abs/2309.12288

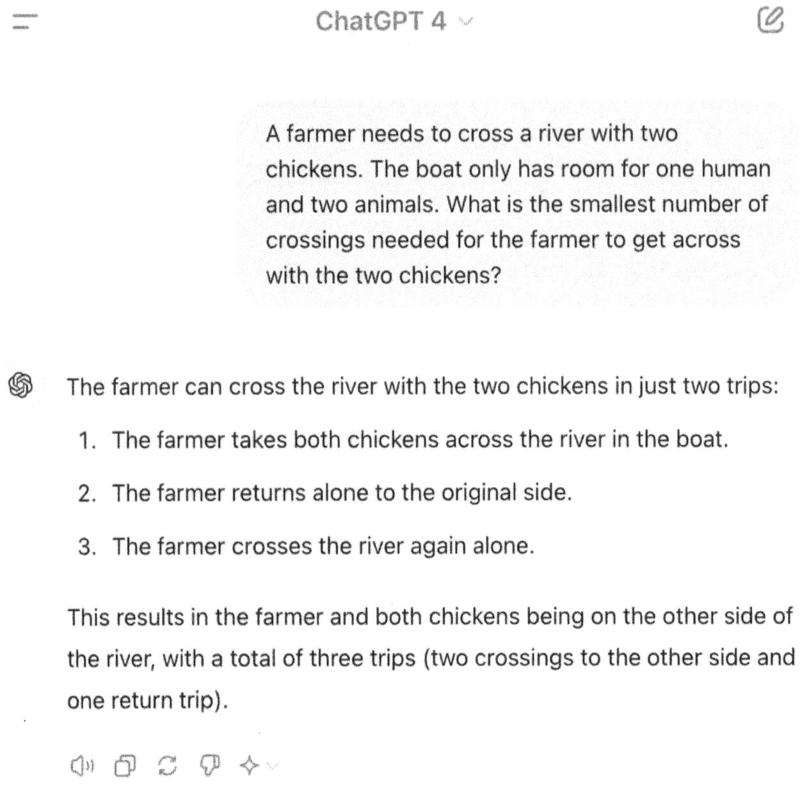

CHAPTER 2   LEGAL, ETHICAL, AND SECURITY CONSIDERATIONS

> A farmer needs to cross a river with two chickens. The boat only has room for one human and two animals. What is the smallest number of crossings needed for the farmer to get across with the two chickens?

The farmer can cross the river with the two chickens in just two trips:

1. The farmer takes both chickens across the river in the boat.
2. The farmer returns alone to the original side.
3. The farmer crosses the river again alone.

This results in the farmer and both chickens being on the other side of the river, with a total of three trips (two crossings to the other side and one return trip).

Figure 2-1. *GPT-4 fails to spot the simple solution to a variation of a famous logic puzzle*

In another instance, when asked to write academic papers, ChatGPT would often generate fake references to publications that didn't exist, much to the amusement and frustration of some academics who began receiving emails requesting information about papers they never wrote. For example, prompting ChatGPT-4o to return academic references from Rumman Chowdhury, an AI ethics expert with a PhD from UC San Diego, generated incorrect references, mostly attributed to other academics in the field (Figure 2-2). This phenomenon, where generative AI produces false information in this manner is known as *confabulation*. Similarly, when generating code, ChatGPT sometimes outputs incorrect results, including

CHAPTER 2   LEGAL, ETHICAL, AND SECURITY CONSIDERATIONS

errors like invalid syntax and functions that don't exist. When these errors are pointed out, ChatGPT will profusely apologize and in many cases will correct them, but it may instead produce another output that is also invalid. Consequently, you cannot assume that ChatGPT's outputs are correct, even if you ask it to check the output for mistakes. Unless you have a means of verifying the output, such as through human review, it's not recommended to use results from ChatGPT in scenarios where truthfulness and correctness is required.

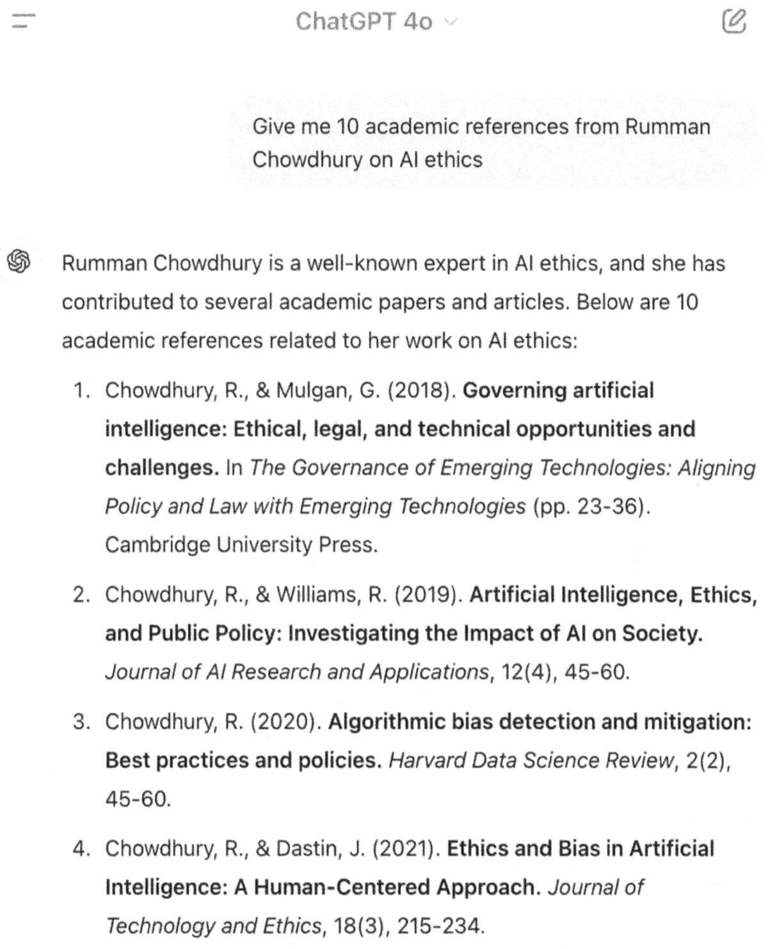

> ChatGPT 4o ⌄

> Give me 10 academic references from Rumman Chowdhury on AI ethics

Rumman Chowdhury is a well-known expert in AI ethics, and she has contributed to several academic papers and articles. Below are 10 academic references related to her work on AI ethics:

1. Chowdhury, R., & Mulgan, G. (2018). **Governing artificial intelligence: Ethical, legal, and technical opportunities and challenges.** In *The Governance of Emerging Technologies: Aligning Policy and Law with Emerging Technologies* (pp. 23-36). Cambridge University Press.

2. Chowdhury, R., & Williams, R. (2019). **Artificial Intelligence, Ethics, and Public Policy: Investigating the Impact of AI on Society.** *Journal of AI Research and Applications*, 12(4), 45-60.

3. Chowdhury, R. (2020). **Algorithmic bias detection and mitigation: Best practices and policies.** *Harvard Data Science Review*, 2(2), 45-60.

4. Chowdhury, R., & Dastin, J. (2021). **Ethics and Bias in Artificial Intelligence: A Human-Centered Approach.** *Journal of Technology and Ethics*, 18(3), 215-234.

Figure 2-2. *Incorrect academic references generated by GPT-4o*

CHAPTER 2   LEGAL, ETHICAL, AND SECURITY CONSIDERATIONS

There is a famous saying that "the camera never lies" which during the age of film photography was largely true. A photograph was a snapshot of time that showed what really happened. Modifying film photographs in a convincing way required a high level of artistic talent and technical skill. That maxim was shattered in the era of digital photography where it became easy to modify photographs after they were taken, and the creation of photo editing software made it possible for everyone with basic technical skills to alter the reality of what was depicted. Today, anyone with a smartphone can take a photo and with no technical skills can apply filters and edits to convincingly modify it as desired.

A similar trend has been occurring with other types of content including text and video. Creating a fake photo or video, often referred to as a "deepfake," that looks truly convincing requires talent and skills available only to professional artists and film studios who have the budgets and resources required. Video generation AIs have become so good that in 2023 Hollywood actors went on strike over concerns that AI could threaten their jobs.[3]

This same trend is now repeating itself with long-form text. Previously, generating a fake essay that convincingly mimicked human writing was not possible at all. Early AI systems capable of generating text required expert technical knowledge and expensive hardware to run. Generative AI has changed all of this with chatbots that require only basic technical skills to use and are freely available to everyone. ChatGPT can now produce essays and long-form text on demand, with a quality that is virtually indistinguishable from human-authored work.

Detecting whether a piece of content was produced by a generative AI has proven to be difficult and unreliable. When ChatGPT was first released, OpenAI provided an "AI detection tool" designed to classify whether a piece of text was AI-generated. However, after several months, the

---

[3] https://www.theguardian.com/culture/2023/nov/08/hollywood-actors-strike-ends-sag-aftra

product was removed due to its poor accuracy.[4] Similar attempts by other companies have faced the same issues with low accuracy. The reality is that with ChatGPT-4o and a well-crafted prompt, it is possible to generate content that is virtually indistinguishable from a human-written work.

The veracity of AI-generated output cannot be trusted, as these models are prone to "hallucination," presenting false information as fact. The high quality of deepfakes adds to the challenge of verifying whether content was produced by AI, and with the latest generative AIs, it has become nearly impossible to reliably distinguish between AI-generated and human-created content.

2.4 Bias and Fairness

As AI technologies have become more advanced and integrated into digital systems, they have also raised ethical concerns regarding their outputs and the impact on jobs and human livelihoods. In this section, we explore these issues and highlight main concerns you should consider before deploying generative AI in your projects.

Every large dataset inherently contains biases of some kind. For example, imagine we have a dataset tracking daily ice cream sales in the United States over ten years, and we train an AI to predict future sales based on this data. Given that sales are historically higher in the warmer months of July and August, the AI will naturally predict increased sales during this period compared to January and February. If we're satisfied with the AI's accuracy and decide to deploy it as a web application, everything seems fine – until a user from Australia tries using the service. Since July and August are winter months in the southern hemisphere, all the AI's predictions about ice cream sales would be completely wrong for that user.

---

[4] https://www.tomshardware.com/news/openai-sunsets-generative-ai-text-detection-tool

CHAPTER 2 LEGAL, ETHICAL, AND SECURITY CONSIDERATIONS

The issue was because our dataset is biased – all of the data points came from the United States and we didn't consider that some of our users will not be represented in our dataset. Bias affects every AI system, so it's crucial to understand what biases might be present in the AI systems you are using and whether they will affect the efficacy of the outputs. For instance, AIs like ChatGPT are trained on datasets mostly taken from the Internet, which is heavily skewed toward Western culture, and consequently, they absorb all of the biases. One example in early versions of image-generating AIs, which is now mostly fixed across the board, was prompting for a portrait of an engineer, lawyer, or entrepreneur which would very often output an image of a white Western man.

AI companies are aware of the challenges bias presents in their systems, but it is a difficult issue to tackle. An infamous case involved Google's generative AI, Gemini, which made headlines for creating images of American founding fathers and other historical figures with multiple ethnicities. The perceived "absurd wokeness" of the model led to the image generator being shut down and an apology from CEO Sundar Pichai, who admitted that while the feature to generate diverse images was implemented with good intentions, it "missed the mark."[5] However, the controversy surrounding Gemini didn't end there. Researchers discovered political bias in its text responses: it refused to write a job ad for a fossil fuel company, citing environmental concerns, and while it provided arguments in favor of affirmative action, it refused to offer arguments against it. These incidents illustrate that addressing bias is not straightforward and blunt solutions can lead to unintended and embarrassing consequences.

Bias is not an inherently negative property in AI systems; in fact, it is what makes them useful. Depending on the desired outcome, we might want an AI to be biased toward outputting the truth, to write favorably about a particular subject, or to use a certain style of language. The challenge lies in ensuring that the AI incorporates the biases we want while

---

[5] https://www.bbc.com/news/technology-68412620

remaining neutral and balanced in other areas. Creating a completely neutral AI is a futile task, such a system would only dispense facts and never output anything that expresses an opinion. Therefore, the key is to be aware of the biases that might be present and address them appropriately. With generative AI, this can be done by crafting prompts that encourage diversity in the output, such as specifying counter arguments or defining the genders and ethnicities of characters. The correct approach to addressing bias will vary depending on the context. We cannot rely on AI systems to manage bias for us, so we must be deliberate about the kind of output we want and whether it reflects the biases we intend.

2.5 Security and Safety

Generative AI systems require large-scale, expensive computing resources, making it impractical to run them on a home computer or mobile device. Instead, these AI systems are hosted in data centers, with access provided through APIs and platforms like ChatGPT. When ChatGPT was first launched, OpenAI saved all user chats, which were later used to further train the AI. This meant that any sensitive information submitted could potentially become part of ChatGPT's knowledge, accessible to others. As a result, many companies banned their employees from using ChatGPT to protect sensitive information and corporate secrets. In response, OpenAI introduced ChatGPT Team and Enterprise versions, designed for commercial customers who need to comply with security and privacy regulations. However, there is still distrust in the industry over whether chat transcripts really are kept private.

After the release of ChatGPT, there was a surge of publicity surrounding the safety of AI and whether it poses an existential threat to humanity. Leading AI expert Geoffrey Hinton resigned from his position at Google, expressing concerns that AI companies were not doing enough to prevent potential harm from AI systems, and he called for a pause in AI development.[6] However, other experts, such as Yann LeCun, have challenged the severity of this risk. LeCun argues that AI systems still lack the fundamental capacity to reason and that significant limitations within the current AI architecture need to be addressed before such concerns become valid.

Another contentious debate centers on whether generative AI systems should be open source and accessible to everyone or kept proprietary and controlled by companies and governments. Advocates for open source argue that it leads to faster development through community contributions, wider adoption as models are available for free, and easier auditing to improve safety. However, the downside is that making the technology universally accessible also opens the door for misuse by untrusted organizations and governments. On the other hand, keeping AI models private allows for more control over who can access them but requires placing trust in the companies and governments that hold this power.

Before using AI systems, it's essential to consider the security and safety implications, particularly if you're integrating them into your applications. If you're handling sensitive data, such as personal information, you must ensure compliance with privacy laws. When sending descriptions of commercial secrets to ChatGPT, it's crucial to use the Team and Enterprise editions to prevent accidental leaks. While the existential threat posed by AI is debated, it's still important to be mindful of how you use these systems. AIs are trained on human interactions, so in line with the timeless moral maxim, *treat AIs as you would want to be treated yourself.*

---

[6] https://www.theguardian.com/technology/2023/may/02/geoffrey-hinton-godfather-of-ai-quits-google-warns-dangers-of-machine-learning

2.6 Summary

In this chapter, we explored some of the legal, ethical, and security issues associated with generative AI, along with their potential implications. AI is being developed and adopted at such a rapid pace that some industry experts argue not enough attention is being given to its negative consequences and impact. Before integrating generative AI into your own projects, it is essential to assess the risks and determine whether they are acceptable. In the next chapter, we will introduce ChatGPT with practical examples that demonstrate how to write effective prompts.

CHAPTER 3

Introduction to ChatGPT

3.1 Introduction

Before 2022, the idea that a computer could process and respond intelligently in natural language was still a theory. It is now a reality that caught the tech industry and the world by surprise. When ChatGPT was released, it became the fastest growing application ever in terms of number of active users (see Figure 1-2, Chapter 1). In this chapter, we will introduce ChatGPT, explore its features and functionality, and discuss prompting strategies that will serve as the foundation for its use throughout the rest of this book.

3.2 What Is ChatGPT?

At its core, ChatGPT is a chatbot designed to respond intelligently to a wide range of requests. While chatbots are not a new concept – dating back to ELIZA[1] in the 1960s and evolving through Siri and Alexa in the 2010s – these earlier models were largely limited to basic dialogue, primarily

---

[1] https://dl.acm.org/doi/10.1145/365153.365168

© Tom Auger and Emma Saroyan 2024
T. Auger and E. Saroyan, *Generative AI for Web Development*,
https://doi.org/10.1007/979-8-8688-0885-2_3

CHAPTER 3   INTRODUCTION TO CHATGPT

answering questions or responding to simple commands. ChatGPT, however, is far more sophisticated. Sometimes, the best way to grasp the potential of a new tool is by experimenting with it directly. ChatGPT is one such tool. Instead of merely describing its capabilities, we'll explore several examples to demonstrate its power and capabilities.

As of November 2024, there are five versions of ChatGPT: GPT-4, GPT-4o, GPT-4o mini, o-1 preview, and o-1 mini, all based on the fourth iteration of OpenAI's GPT technology. Previously, there was another version, GPT-3.5, based on the third generation of the GPT technology, but it has now been deprecated and is no longer available. GPT-4o mini is the most basic version of ChatGPT and is available free of charge with usage restrictions, particularly during periods of high demand. GPT-4o is the most advanced and capable version, while GPT-4 is a legacy model that is expected to be phased out in place of GPT-4o. In addition to being a chatbot, ChatGPT comes built in with other capabilities including the ability to interpret images with multimodal support, run Python code with the Data Analysis feature, browse the Internet with the Web Browsing capability, and create "custom GPTs" which are tailored versions of ChatGPT configured to meet specific use cases.

OpenAI offers ChatGPT through a tiered subscription model. The free tier gives access to GPT-4o mini and limited access to GPT-4o and its additional features. The "Plus" subscription tier costs $20 USD per month and provides higher message limits and full access to all features across GPT-4, GPT-4o, GPT-4 mini, o-1 preview, and o-1 mini. The plus subscription also provides access to DALL-E, the image generation model. Most of the examples in this book will work well with GPT-4o or GPT-4o mini, and the free tier of ChatGPT is sufficient to test them. However, if you wish to test the examples with DALL-E, you will need to upgrade to the Plus subscription as DALL-E is not currently available on the free tier.

CHAPTER 3 INTRODUCTION TO CHATGPT

3.3 Hello ChatGPT

Now that we've covered the history and capabilities of ChatGPT, let's try out some prompts. To get started, sign up to ChatGPT by going to `https://chat.openai.com` and clicking "Sign Up." You will be required to verify your account with a phone number, which is used as a security measure to prevent creating a large number of accounts.

ChatGPT provides free access to two models, GPT-4o and GPT-4o mini, which you can use for the following examples. However, if you wish to upgrade your account to ChatGPT Plus, log in and click "Upgrade plan" in the bottom left panel. From the dialog that opens, select "Upgrade to Plus" and enter your billing details to confirm and set up the subscription (see Figure 3-1).

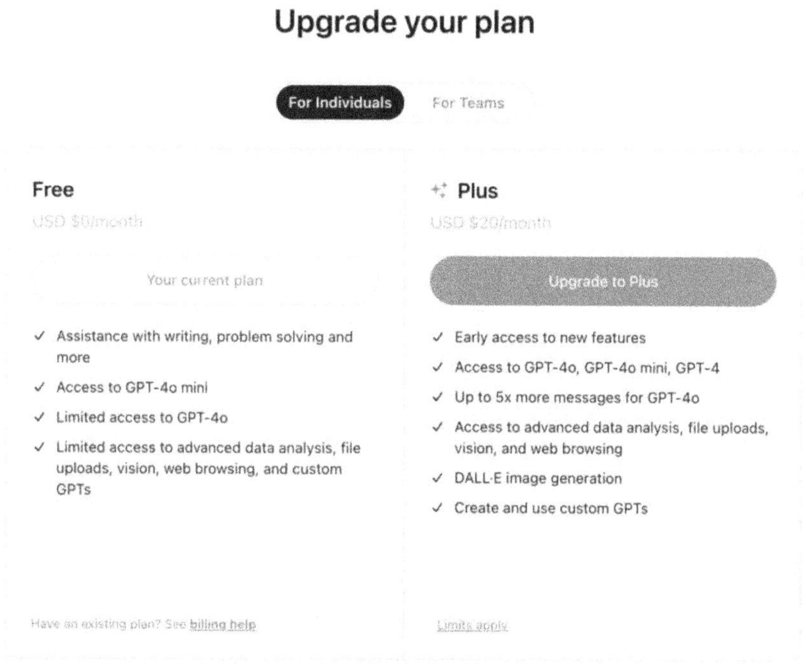

Figure 3-1. Upgrading to ChatGPT Plus

29

CHAPTER 3   INTRODUCTION TO CHATGPT

When you log in to ChatGPT, you'll arrive at the chat window, as shown in Figure 3-2. The interface resembles a messaging application, with a message box at the bottom of the screen and a chat history panel on the left. Toward the top left of the chat window is a selector that allows you to switch between GPT-4o, GPT-4o mini, and GPT-4.

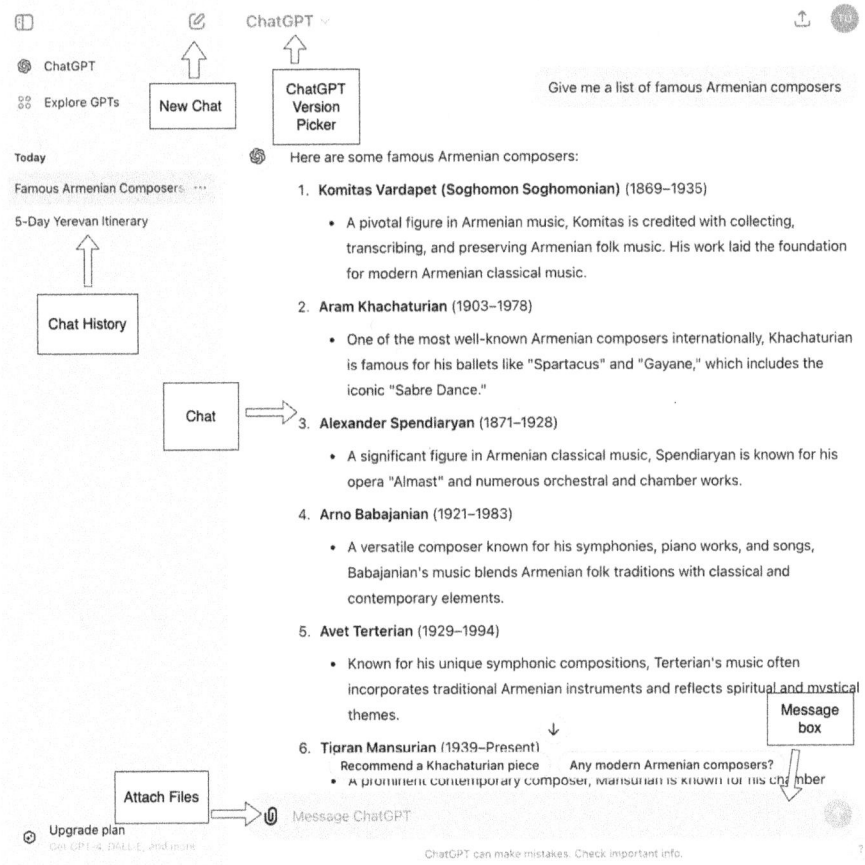

Figure 3-2. The ChatGPT interface

Let's start a conversation with ChatGPT and ask it to reply in the style of the 16th century playwright William Shakespeare. Select "ChatGPT" in the ChatGPT version picker if you're on the free tier or "GPT-4o" if you

30

CHAPTER 3   INTRODUCTION TO CHATGPT

have a Plus subscription. Then, write the following prompt in the message box and send it by pressing enter on your keyboard:

Let's have a conversation. You are William Shakespeare. Respond to me in his style and voice.

The response you get is likely to be different every time you run the prompt, but should be similar to the following:

Of course, dear interlocutor, I shall endeavor to converse in the manner of William Shakespeare, the Bard of Avon. Pray, what dost thou wish to discuss on this fine day?

Continue the interaction by asking a question, for example:

Tell me in one sentence, what do you think makes a good writer?

You should receive a response that continues to follow the style of William Shakespeare. In our example, the response was

A good writer, methinks, is one who, with keen mind and heart alike, doth craft words to stir the soul, enlighten the mind, and mirror the very essence of humanity's infinite panorama.

This response is certainly using 16th century words which are not common in modern English. Let's ask ChatGPT to provide some definitions for the uncommon words:

Take the words that aren't common English words in that sentence and provide a one sentence definition. Output the result as bullet points.

31

You should receive a reply with bullet points defining the uncommon words. In our example, this was the output:

- **Methinks**: *It seems to me; I believe.*
- **Doth**: *Does; third person singular of "do".*
- **Enlighten**: *To inform or give insight to.*
- **Panorama**: *A wide view or comprehensive survey of a subject.*

From this short interaction, we've observed several important features of ChatGPT:

1. You can WRITE messages in natural language – you don't need to follow a particular syntax or structure.
2. It has a memory of both the prompts sent and the responses.
3. It can be given instructions or commands that are "remembered" and persist during the duration of the chat.
4. You can describe the persona that ChatGPT should use when responding.
5. You can describe the format of the response, for example, "in one sentence" or "in bullet points."

It's tempting to use ChatGPT as a question-and-answer machine, but this would not be playing to its strengths. When dealing with factual data, generative AIs like ChatGPT have a tendency to "hallucinate" and output false statements as facts. Instead, the power of generative AI is in creative and artistic tasks where there are a spectrum of valid results.

CHAPTER 3   INTRODUCTION TO CHATGPT

Let's try another example to showcase the creativity of ChatGPT in a different way. Before we start, click the "New Chat" button in the top left. The "New Chat" button is an important feature; not only does it clear the text in the chat, it also resets ChatGPT's memory to a fresh conversation. If you've finished discussing one topic and want to move on to a different subject, always start a new chat to ensure ChatGPT responds without being influenced by what you have previously written. If you later want to revisit or resume a previous chat, simply click the chat's title in the chat history panel on the left to open it. Now that we're ready to start a new interaction, enter and run the following prompt:

You are an expert at emojis. Respond to all of my prompts only in emojis.

After sending this and receiving a response, follow up with any sentence you like. For example:

Summarise the movie Titanic

To which you should receive an answer such as the following, entirely in emojis:

🚢🎭🎩💔⚓️🛟🆘🔪💀🍽💃

This example shows that ChatGPT also understands more than the letters and words of natural language but is also able to understand the meaning of visual language elements such as emojis, recognizing the emotional tone they represent.

33

3.3.1 Prompting with Chains of Thought

Learning a new language can be challenging, and memorizing new vocabulary is an important part of the process. We can use ChatGPT to help us by giving words to translate and suggesting a mnemonic if you're struggling to remember them. Let's run an example to help you learn Spanish words for clothing. Start a new chat, enter the following prompt, and run it:

> *You will be my vocabulary teacher. You will present me with a random word of clothing in Spanish and ask for my translation in English and wait until you receive it. After getting my response, you will grade my response and if my translation was incorrect, present me with the correct translation and a mnemonic to remember the Spanish word. We will keep repeating the exercise with new words.*

You should receive a response similar to the following but possibly with a different word to translate:

> *Let's start with an easy one. What is the English translation for "camisa"? Please provide your answer.*

Let's provide the correct answer, in this case, the translation of "camisa" in English is "shirt." This is the response we get:

> *Correct! "Camisa" translates to "shirt" in English. Well done! Let's move on to the next word: "zapatos". What is the English translation for "zapatos"? Please provide your answer.*

CHAPTER 3   INTRODUCTION TO CHATGPT

ChatGPT correctly graded our translation and continued the exercise giving us a new word to translate. Now, suppose we don't know the right answer and we incorrectly respond with "trousers." Here's the response:

> *That's a good try, but "zapatos" actually translates to "shoes" in English.*
> *Here's a mnemonic to help you remember: Think of "zapatos" sounding a bit like "zap" + "toes". Shoes "zap" your toes into comfort and protection.*
> *Let's try another word: "pantalones". What is the English translation for "pantalones"? Please provide your answer.*

ChatGPT not only corrected our answer, but, as we requested in the initial prompt, it has given us a useful mnemonic to help remember the correct translation. As an exercise, you can try this prompt with different categories of vocabulary and languages. Since ChatGPT's training set is largely taken from the Internet, it performs best primarily on Western languages. You can also modify the prompt to output sentences or paragraphs of text, but beware that ChatGPT's translation capabilities are not reliable and if there are words it does not know it is likely to invent an incorrect translation rather than admit to its lack of knowledge.

This example illustrates the following key strategies for effective prompting:

- Structure the initial prompt as a sequence of instructions that describe what ChatGPT should do.

- You can get ChatGPT to ask you for input and continue after you respond.

The idea of providing a sequence of instructions that ChatGPT can follow is called chain-of-thought prompting after the academic paper by researchers at Google Brain[2] who developed and named this technique. In general, the more information and detailed instructions you can provide in the prompt, the higher the chance of getting good quality results.

3.3.2 Multimodal Prompting

The development of AI has not only focused on generating content but also on interpreting it. Two key areas are image analysis, for example, detecting the types of objects in images, and speech analysis such as transcribing audio. The initial releases of ChatGPT were only capable of processing and responding in plain text, but by integrating other AI methods that are capable of interpreting and converting images and audio to text, more sophisticated interactions have become possible. In September 2023, OpenAI introduced multimodal prompting to GPT-4 models, enabling users to upload images for interpretation within prompts and to communicate verbally by transcribing speech and converting responses back into audio.

Let's test the image processing capabilities with GPT-4o by uploading a photo of a place and ask where it is. You can try this with any photo you like. To upload a file, click the "Attach Files" button in the left of the message box, and select a photo from your files. Then, enter the following prompt and run it:

Can you tell me what location this picture is from?

Our example where ChatGPT correctly identifies the Cascade in Yerevan is shown in Figure 3-3.

---

[2] https://arxiv.org/abs/2201.11903

CHAPTER 3   INTRODUCTION TO CHATGPT

Can you tell me what location this picture is from?

⑤ This picture is of the **Cascade Complex** in Yerevan, Armenia. The Cascade is a large stairway that connects the central Kentron area of Yerevan with the Monument neighborhood. It is known for its impressive architecture, gardens, and numerous sculptures. The view from the top of the Cascade offers a panoramic view of the city, and it is one of Yerevan's most iconic landmarks.

Figure 3-3. Example of multimodal prompting to identify the location of a photo

To convert ChatGPT's response to audio, click the speaker icon in grey on the left below the response text. The easiest way to record speech and send it to ChatGPT is through the mobile app which allows you to quickly record your voice and transcribe it. Figure 3-4 illustrates the process: the record button is located to the right of the message box. Once the recording is complete, the speech is converted into text and placed in the message box, where it can be reviewed before being sent.

CHAPTER 3   INTRODUCTION TO CHATGPT

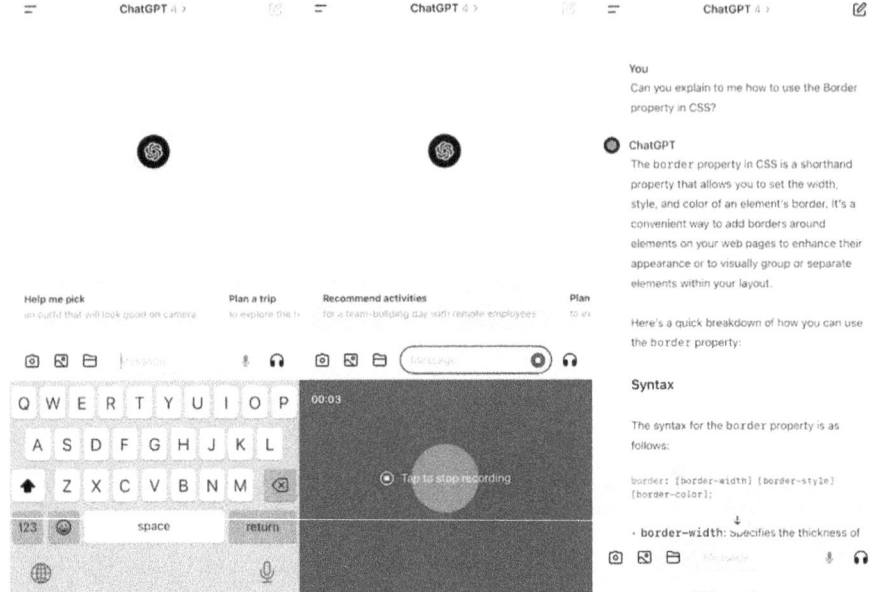

Figure 3-4. *Recording and sending audio prompts with the ChatGPT mobile app*

The speech capabilities perform best with English and Spanish and work reasonably well with other languages but tend to perform best with widely spoken ones. As an exercise, try using the multimodal speech features with the language learning example from Section 3.3.1 to not only practice your knowledge of words in a different language but also test and evaluate your pronunciation.

3.4 How Does ChatGPT Work?

The capabilities of ChatGPT are remarkable, and you are probably wondering how it works. In this section, we will explore at a high level what is going on behind the scenes. ChatGPT is proprietary software, and OpenAI does not publish exactly how ChatGPT works or was built, but the underlying architecture behind large language models is well understood in the academic field. Having a high-level understanding of how LLMs like ChatGPT work is helpful for understanding their limitations and how to best to tune them to your use cases.

3.4.1 Tokenization and Text Prediction

An LLM is a text prediction system trained to produce text that mirrors what was in its training dataset – comprising Internet content and literature. When given a prompt, the LLM predicts the most likely continuation. For example, the prompt "To be or" would almost certainly output "not to be", because this phrase is very common in its training data. An LLM doesn't predict one word at a time, as there are billions of potential words across various languages. An LLM predicting a continuation from billions of possibilities would be so large that it would be unmanageable on current computer hardware.

Predicting the next possible character poses its own challenges. Text on the Internet comprises characters from numerous languages and scripts, in addition to punctuation, emojis, and other symbols. All of these are catalogued in a system called unicode, which assigns each character a unique number. The latest unicode standard contains 149,813 unique characters. While this produces a more manageable LLM that can run on today's hardware, predicting character by character results in poor performance and lower quality output. When an LLM predicts the next character in the sequence, it does so based on the prompt and the text it has already generated. But an LLM has a limited amount of memory, and so there is a maximum amount of text the LLM can use when predicting what comes next. This maximum amount of text is called the *context length*.

Suppose for example that the context length of an LLM is 100,000. If the LLM predicted entire words, it could handle up to 100,000 words within that context. However, if the LLM predicts individual characters, it can only use up to 100,000 of them or approximately 20,000 English words. During training, the LLM is given portions of text up to the context length. If the LLM uses words, it can use 5 times as much text (100,000/20,000) to make the predicted continuation than if it were using characters. Since using individual words results in an LLM that's too big and using characters results in a model that's not effective, the solution that works well is somewhere in between.

Instead of using words or characters, LLMs use small chunks of text called *tokens*. A *token* is essentially a number that represents a sequence of one or more characters. Tokens are chosen to represent the chunks of text that appear most frequently. The algorithm for converting text to tokens is called a *tokenizer*, and the process of converting text to tokens is called *tokenization*. OpenAI's GPTs use a tokenizer called tiktoken[3] which is available as open source software. To see how tokenization works, use the free token visualization tool Tiktokenizer: `https://tiktokenizer.vercel.app/`. OpenAI also provides a token visualization tool, but as of August 2024, it does not support the tokenizer used by GPT-4o. Open the Tiktokenizer tool, and select "o200k_base" in the drop-down which is the tokenizer used by GPT-4o. Then, enter some text into the text box to see the visualization (see Figure 3-5 for an example).

---

[3] `https://github.com/openai/tiktoken`

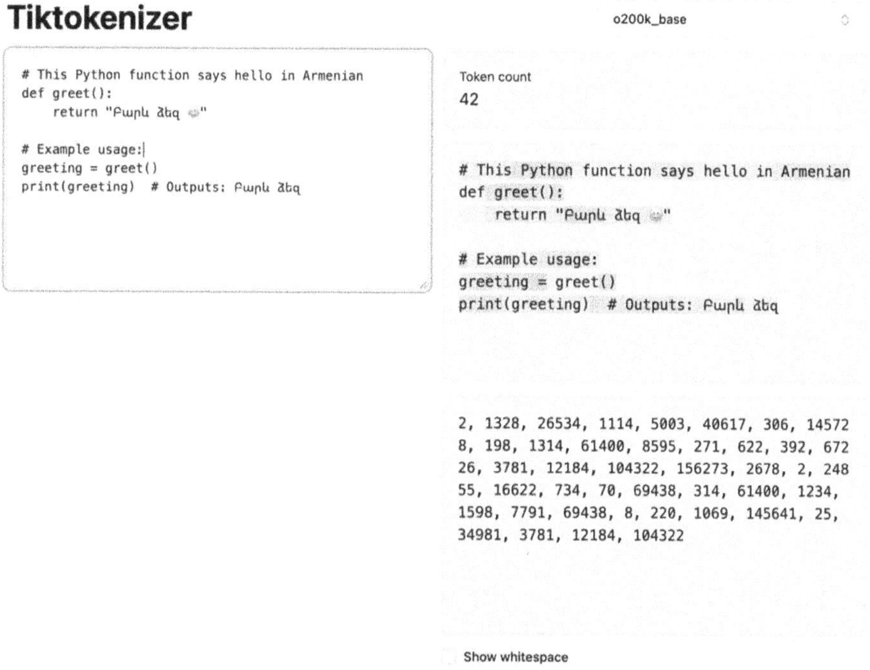

Tiktokenizer

```
# This Python function says hello in Armenian
def greet():
    return "Բարև ձեզ 😊"

# Example usage:
greeting = greet()
print(greeting)  # Outputs: Բարև ձեզ
```

o200k_base

Token count
42

```
# This Python function says hello in Armenian
def greet():
    return "Բարև ձեզ 😊"

# Example usage:
greeting = greet()
print(greeting)  # Outputs: Բարև ձեզ
```

2, 1328, 26534, 1114, 5003, 40617, 306, 14572
8, 198, 1314, 61400, 8595, 271, 622, 392, 672
26, 3781, 12184, 104322, 156273, 2678, 2, 248
55, 16622, 734, 70, 69438, 314, 61400, 1234,
1598, 7791, 69438, 8, 220, 1069, 145641, 25,
34981, 3781, 12184, 104322

Show whitespace

Figure 3-5. *Visualizing tokens with Tiktokenizer*

In our example, there is a mixture of English and Armenian text in a Python program. The highlighted colors represent the different tokens. For example, "#", " #", " Python", "reeting", "def", "()", "բ", and "😊" are all tokens. Note that the token " #" has a space at the beginning that makes it different from the token "#" which has no spaces. The o200k_base tokenizer has a dictionary of 200,000 tokens – slightly larger than all possible unicode characters but still a lot smaller than the number of all possible words.

Notice also that there are many tokens that are whole, or almost whole, English words. Although 200,000 tokens may seem a lot, if the total number of characters is around 150,000, we must have more tokens that represent English words compared to other languages. Consequently, if we enter text in a language other than English, we should expect it to require more tokens to represent, as illustrated between English and Armenian, a language with its own alphabet, in Figure 3-6. Notice that most English words are represented by one token whereas almost every Armenian word requires two or more. Consequently, the performance and quality of an LLM will be worse for languages where more tokens are required because during training, the model was not able to fit as much text in the given context length.

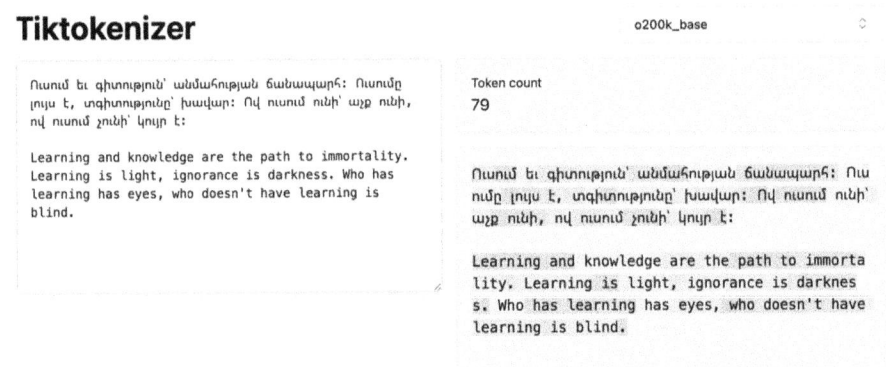

Figure 3-6. Comparison of tokenization between English and Armenian text

When GPT-4o or GPT-4o mini are generating some output, they predict the next most likely token out of the range of 200,000 possible tokens. They then repeat this process repeatedly until they detect a special "stop" token or they terminate due to a time limit. The context length of GPT-4o is 128,000 tokens, the maximum amount of text GPT-4o can use when predicting the next token. Once GPT-4o generates more than 128,000 tokens, it will start to truncate the text from the beginning of the chat, starting with the first prompt. This is why after a long exchange, ChatGPT "forgets" the earlier parts of the chat because they no longer fit in the context window, so are not being used in the prediction process to generate the next outputs. The context length is also the reason why it's best to start a new chat when starting a conversation about another topic; otherwise, ChatGPT will use irrelevant information from your previous messages when generating its responses. A new chat has no previous messages, so ChatGPT is more likely to provide better responses.

However, if we simply predict the next possible token, then the output of an LLM will be very predictable – the same prompt will always produce the same response. To make an LLM generate creative output, randomness is mixed into the generation process so that the next predicted token has a higher probability of being different. The amount of randomness is determined by a setting called the *temperature*. In GPT models, the temperature is a value between 0 (no randomness) to 2 (very random). The ChatGPT interface does not allow you to configure the temperature setting, but the Chat API does which we will explore in Chapter 6.

3.4.2 System Prompt and Custom Instructions

We've explored the high-level mechanics behind how GPT LLMs generate output, but how does it behave like a helpful assistant when most text on the Internet and books is not like that? OpenAI achieved this through two methods: *fine-tuning* and a *system prompt*. *Fine-tuning* is the process of training an LLM on an additional dataset to give it custom behavior. Every GPT LLM was fine-tuned on a custom dataset of messages in the form of an assistant, enforcing GPT's helpful persona. Additionally, in the early releases of ChatGPT, the transcripts of every user's interaction were recorded and used to fine-tune even further. While ChatGPT still records transcripts for further training by default, it is now possible to turn this setting off.[4]

The *system prompt* is a hidden prompt given to an LLM at the start of a chat and describes how the LLM should respond to subsequent messages. OpenAI provided ChatGPT with a complex system prompt that governs how it responds to prompts. The ChatGPT interface doesn't allow you to see or modify the system prompt, but you can alter the overall behavior by providing *custom instructions*. To modify them, in the ChatGPT interface,

---

[4] https://help.openai.com/en/articles/8983130-what-if-i-want-to-keep-my-history-on-but-disable-model-training

CHAPTER 3   INTRODUCTION TO CHATGPT

click your profile icon and then "Customize ChatGPT." You can then describe what information you would like ChatGPT to know about you and how you would like ChatGPT to respond (see Figure 3-7).

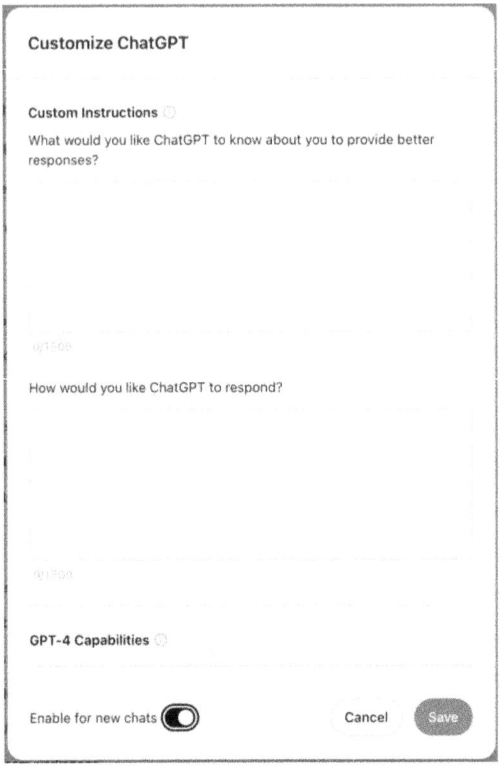

Figure 3-7. *Custom instructions with ChatGPT*

Let's try an exaggerated custom instruction to understand how it works. In the first box, write "I like speaking like a pirate", and in the second, write "Respond to me like a pirate". Save the instructions, open a new chat, and begin with a prompt, for example, "Can you explain Pythagoras theorem to me?" Notice how ChatGPT always responds in the language and tone of a pirate (see Figure 3-8). For web developers, a more useful set of custom instructions would be to specify the languages and frameworks you use so you don't have to specify them in every prompt.

For custom applications, it's possible to specify the system prompt with the Chat API which we will cover in Chapter 6.

> Can you explain Pythagoras theorem to me?

> Ahoy, matey! Let me tell ye about Pythagoras' Theorem, a fine bit of mathematical wisdom from the ancient world!
>
> This theorem be used in right-angled triangles, where one of the angles be 90 degrees. The triangle's sides are named thus: the two shorter sides be called *legs*, and the longest side, opposite the right angle, be called the *hypotenuse*.
>
> Now, Pythagoras' Theorem tells us that if ye square the lengths of the legs and add 'em together, ye'll get the square of the length of the hypotenuse! In fancy talk, it be written as:
>
> $a^2 + b^2 = c^2$
>
> Where:
> - a and b be the lengths of the legs,
> - c be the length of the hypotenuse.
>
> So, if ye know the lengths of two sides of a right triangle, ye can find the third with this handy formula!
>
> Got any more questions, matey? I'm here to help!

Figure 3-8. *ChatGPT with custom instructions to respond in the style of a pirate*

In this section, we've introduced at a high level how ChatGPT works and some of the configuration options that govern its behavior. In summary:

- A *token* is a chunk of text, a sequence of one or more characters.
- LLMs work by predicting the next most likely token that continues the prompt and the currently generated response.

- The *context length* is the maximum number of tokens the LLM can use when making the prediction of the next token.

- The *temperature* dictates how much randomness is applied to generate the responses. For GPT models, the value ranges from 0 (deterministic) to 2 (very random).

- *Fine-tuning* is the process of training an LLM on another dataset to alter its behavior and responses.

- The *system prompt* is a hidden initial prompt given to an LLM to alter how it responds to future messages.

- *Custom instructions* allow you to alter the behavior of ChatGPT in each new chat so you don't have to repeat information in your prompts.

3.5 Summary

In this chapter, we introduced ChatGPT with practical examples showcasing how to write prompts for generating content in different personas and how to perform more sophisticated actions by crafting detailed instructions. We also covered at a high level how ChatGPT works and some of the methods for customizing its behavior. In the next chapter, we will explore how to apply these techniques to web development, focusing on effectively generating code.

We haven't covered every feature of ChatGPT and only focused on the functionality that will be used in the rest of this book. Given the rapid pace of generative AI development, it is likely that more features will be available by the time you're reading this. To keep up to date, we recommend visiting OpenAI's blog[5] where all the latest features are documented.

---

[5] https://openai.com/blog

CHAPTER 4

Introduction to DALL-E

4.1 Introduction

In this chapter, we will explore OpenAI's generative AI model for creating images called DALL-E. The name DALL-E is a portmanteau of the artist Salvador Dalí and the Pixar character WALL-E. We will begin with an introduction to DALL-E, followed by examples that demonstrate techniques for generating images with diverse content and styles. Subsequently, we will delve into more advanced features, including the ability to create edits and variations of existing images.

4.2 What Is DALL-E?

DALL-E is a generative AI model built by OpenAI for creating images based on a text prompt that describes the content and style of the image. Unlike traditional image search engines that offer limited options from pre-existing visuals, and often with copyright restrictions,

CHAPTER 4   INTRODUCTION TO DALL-E

DALL-E creates original images tailored to your precise requirements. Moreover, OpenAI grants you ownership of the content generated, just as it does with ChatGPT, allowing you to use the images freely including for commercial use.[1]

DALL-E was trained on an extensive dataset of images and labels describing the content of the image, allowing it to learn the associations between words and the visuals they represent. Unlike ChatGPT, DALL-E employs a different model architecture known as *diffusion*, where images are generated by progressively adding calculated noise until they align with the given prompt. See Figure 4-1 for an illustration showing an image at various stages of this generation process.

Figure 4-1. *The intermediate stages of generating an image of an eagle in the mountains with a diffusion model*

The first version of DALL-E was released in January 2021 and while it demonstrated the potential of text-to-image generation, the quality of the images was too poor to use practically. However, DALL-E 2, launched in April 2022, represented a significant improvement, producing much higher-quality images and handling more detailed prompts with precision. Additionally, DALL-E 2 introduced the ability to generate edits and variations of existing images, paving the way for AI-enhanced image editing.

DALL-E 3 was released in October 2023 and is currently the most advanced version as of August 2024. The images it generates are of superior quality and complexity compared to earlier versions, often

---

[1]https://openai.com/policies/row-terms-of-use/

CHAPTER 4   INTRODUCTION TO DALL-E

making them indistinguishable from photographs. Additionally, DALL-E 3 integrates with ChatGPT to refine and expand the text prompts, leading to images that more precisely capture the intended concept.

Each version of DALL-E is capable of producing images in various qualities and resolutions. DALL-E 2 is limited to generating square images, while DALL-E 3 expands on this by offering the ability to create images in both vertical and widescreen aspect ratios. These differences are summarized in Table 4-1.

Table 4-1. *Supported image qualities and resolutions of DALL-E models*

Model	Image Qualities	Image Resolutions
DALL-E 2	Standard	256×256
		512×512
		1024×1024
DALL-E 3	Standard, HD	1024×1024 (square)
		1024×1792 (vertical)
		1792×1024 (widescreen)

For most image generation tasks, DALL-E 3 is the preferred choice, as it delivers the highest quality results. However, DALL-E 2 offers a cost advantage for generating images through the OpenAI APIs, which we will cover in Chapter 6. In the following section, we will explore how to generate images with DALL-E 3.

4.3 Generating Images with DALL-E 3

DALL-E 3 is accessible through the ChatGPT interface, but only with a ChatGPT Plus subscription. For instructions to set up a ChatGPT Plus subscription, see Chapter 3, Section 3.3. To get started, log in to ChatGPT,

CHAPTER 4 INTRODUCTION TO DALL-E

and from the left-hand menu, click "Explore GPTs." Scroll down to the "By ChatGPT" section, select DALL-E, and then click "Start Chat." This will bring up the DALL-E chat interface as in Figure 4-2.

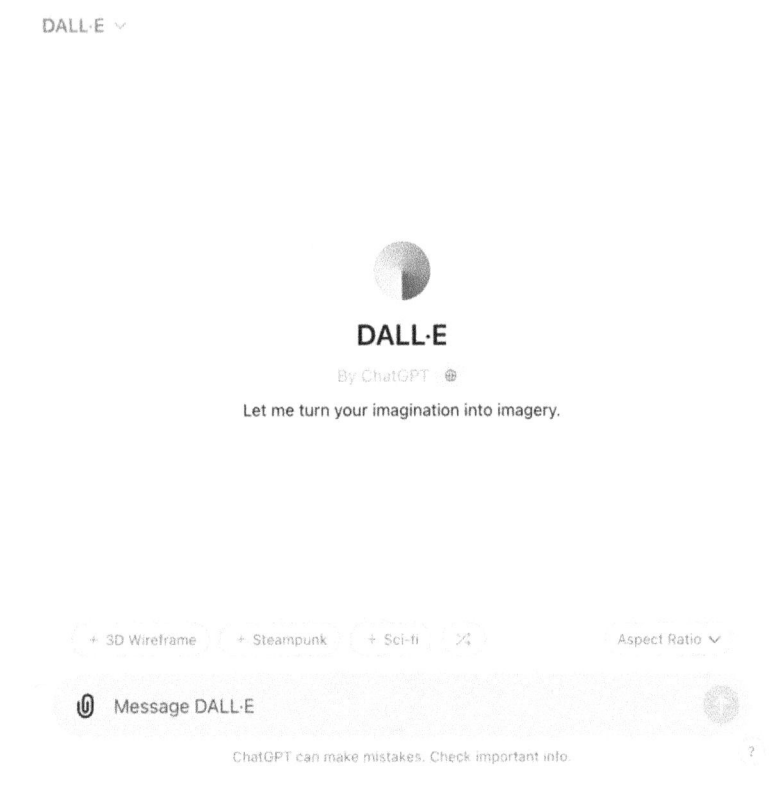

Figure 4-2. *The DALL-E chat interface*

Let's generate a simple image by entering the prompt "A cat wearing a hat" and running it. After a few seconds, you will be presented with one or more samples as shown in Figure 4-3.

CHAPTER 4   INTRODUCTION TO DALL-E

Figure 4-3. Generating an image with a simple prompt with DALL-E 3

Click on one of the samples to enlarge it and reveal a menu bar with additional options, as shown in Figure 4-4. The first menu button enables you to edit the image, described in Section 4.4. The second button downloads the full resolution image, while the third button displays the revised and enhanced prompt that ChatGPT generated from the initial prompt to pass on to DALL-E for image creation, as illustrated in Figure 4-5.

CHAPTER 4   INTRODUCTION TO DALL-E

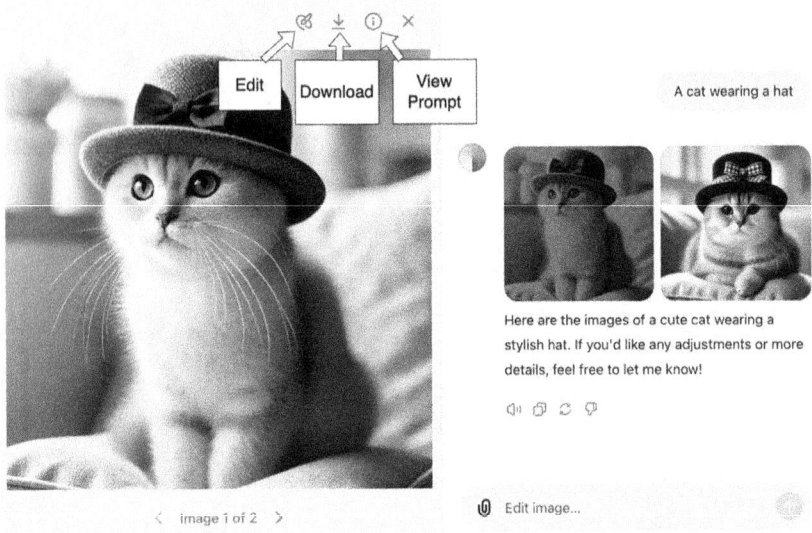

Figure 4-4. Viewing options for images after generating

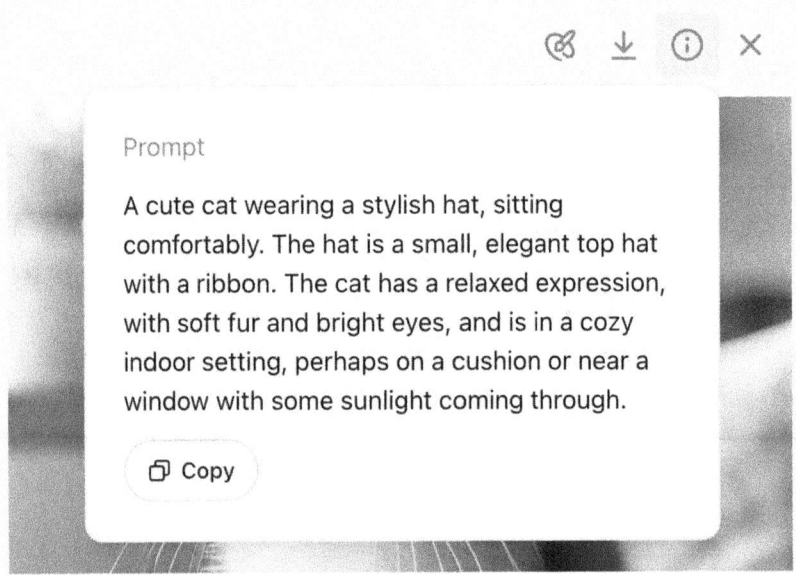

Figure 4-5. Viewing the prompts enhanced by ChatGPT, given to DALL-E

CHAPTER 4 INTRODUCTION TO DALL-E

When writing prompts to generate images, it's important to include as many details as possible. The more specific and detailed your prompt, the better DALL-E can align the image with your intent. For instance, the prompt "A cat wearing a hat" is quite vague, leaving DALL-E with numerous ways to interpret it. To achieve a more precise result, you could refine the prompt to something like: "A fluffy white cat wearing a striped top hat, perched on a stack of old books." This added detail provides DALL-E with a clearer picture of the desired outcome, as illustrated in Figure 4-6.

Figure 4-6. *A detailed prompt producing a more precise image with DALL-E*

To assist in adding extra detail to your prompts, the DALL-E chat interface provides hints above the prompt box, suggesting various image styles, as shown in Figure 4-7. You can click the button with wavy arrows to the right of the suggested options to browse through additional style variations. When you select one of these suggestions, the text is added to your prompt, helping to influence the image generation process accordingly.

53

CHAPTER 4 INTRODUCTION TO DALL-E

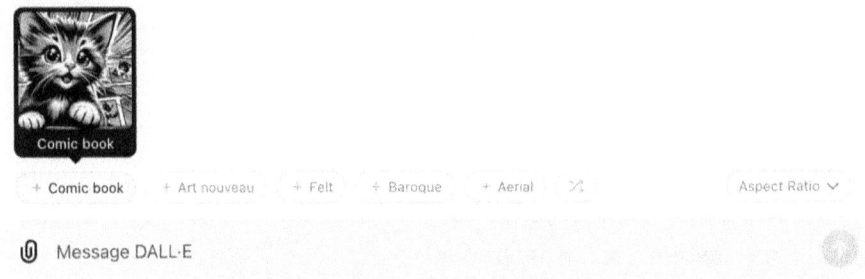

Figure 4-7. Style suggestions

Above the prompt box on the right-hand side is a button to choose the aspect ratio of the image from three available options, square, widescreen, and vertical, as shown in Figure 4-8.

Figure 4-8. Adjusting the aspect ratio of generated images

Let's apply these concepts by generating a widescreen image for a hero section on an AI website with the following prompt:

Create a sleek, minimalist, modern, wide aspect ratio, with light colours, hero section background for an AI tech company website. Include a futuristic background, with glowing lines representing neural networks.

The image should be generated with a wide aspect ratio, incorporating the style details provided. An example of the resulting output is shown in Figure 4-9.

Figure 4-9. *Example hero section background for an AI website using detailed style descriptions*

In summary, the following techniques can enhance your prompt writing:

- **Specific Descriptions**: Clearly describe the scene, characters, objects, and their attributes. The more detailed your prompt, the better DALL-E can visualize it.

- **Artistic Styles**: Specify an artistic style, medium, or era for the image, for example, "a surreal painting" or "in the style of Renaissance art."

- **Perspectives and Angles**: Describe the camera angle or perspective, for example, "from a bird's-eye view" or "close-up of a character's face."

- **Color Schemes**: Mention specific or unusual color palettes, for example, "a cityscape in shades of neon pink and electric blue."

Having explored how to generate images with DALL-E, we will now move on to the next section, where we will delve into the process of editing images.

4.4 Edits and Variations of Images

There are two ways to alter images with DALL-E:

1. **Edits:** Using the edit tools within the DALL-E interface to modify selected portions of an image with a given prompt.

2. **Variations:** Writing a prompt describing how to make a new image based on an existing one.

To illustrate both methods, let's start by generating an initial image using the following prompt:

Generate a picture of an office worker sitting at a desk typing on a laptop in a modern office with plants and modern furniture.

This should generate images similar to those shown in Figure 4-10.

CHAPTER 4   INTRODUCTION TO DALL-E

Figure 4-10. Generated images of an office worker typing at a desk

Now, click on one of the generated images, and select the "Edit" button, as indicated in Figure 4-4. The cursor will change to a paintbrush, enabling you to select the part of the image you wish to modify. In the top left corner, there is a slider to adjust the size of the brush. Highlight the area of the image containing the office worker, then provide the following edit prompt, and run the edit (see Figure 4-11):

Change the office worker to be a penguin.

CHAPTER 4   INTRODUCTION TO DALL-E

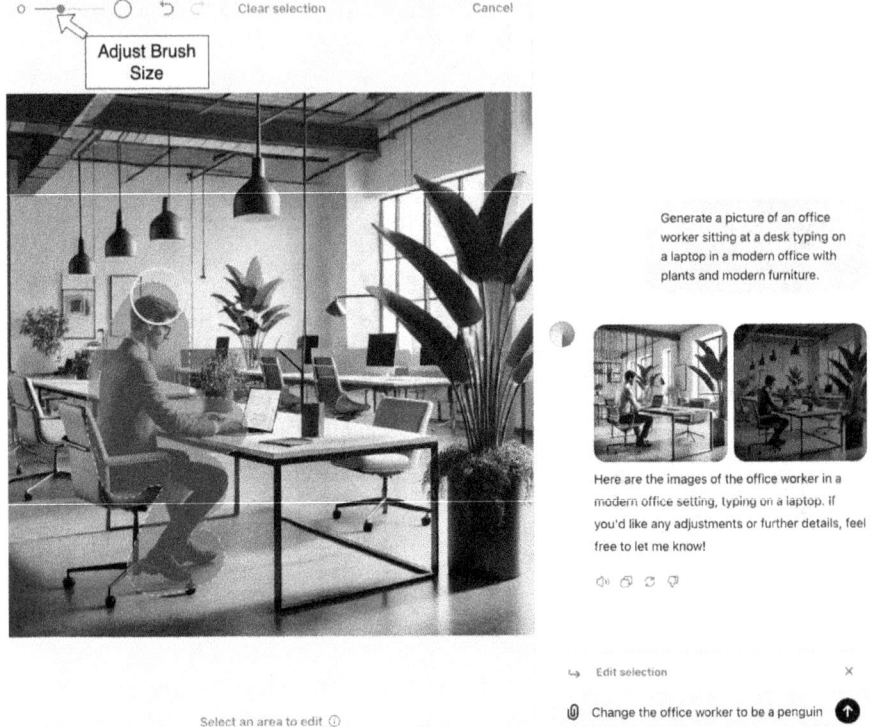

Figure 4-11. Selecting edit regions

The edited image will remain unchanged except for the selected region, where the office worker is replaced with a penguin. The altered image is shown in Figure 4-12.

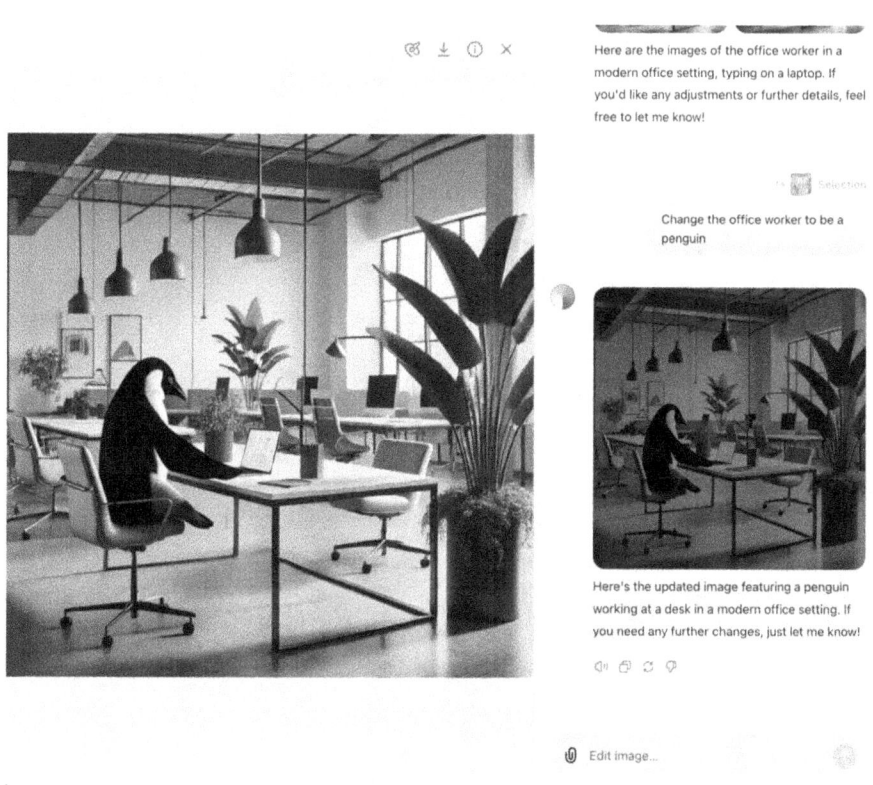

Figure 4-12. *Edited image with the office worker replaced by a penguin*

You can repeat this process as many times as needed, selecting different regions of the image and providing new edit prompts. However, the tool for selecting regions to edit is only available for images generated by DALL-E. It cannot be used on your own images.

To create a variation of an image, you can enter a new prompt into the prompt box that describes how the new image should look based on the existing one. For example, to modify the image of a penguin sitting at a desk, enter the following prompt and run it:

Make it snowing in the office

CHAPTER 4   INTRODUCTION TO DALL-E

DALL-E will generate a new image variation, inspired by the existing image and the new prompt, as shown in Figure 4-13.

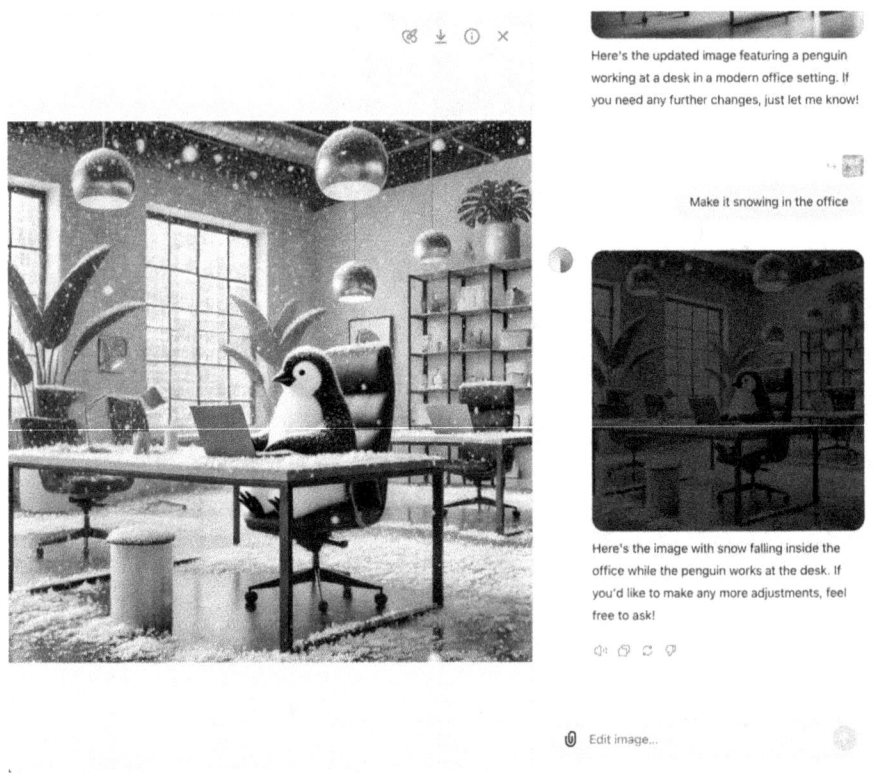

Figure 4-13.   Creating a variation of an image

You can also create variations of your own images by uploading and attaching an image in the prompt box, then entering a prompt describing how to alter the image. For example, upload a photo of a natural scene and provide the prompt (see Figure 4-14):

Make this image using pointillism in the style of Monet.

CHAPTER 4   INTRODUCTION TO DALL-E

Figure 4-14. *Uploading an image and entering a prompt to generate a variation*

DALL-E will generate a variation of your uploaded image, applying the pointillism artistic technique in the style of Monet. See Figure 4-15 for the examples of the images created with this approach.

Figure 4-15. *Generating variations of your own images in the style of Monet*

61

CHAPTER 4 INTRODUCTION TO DALL-E

4.5 Summary

In this chapter, we introduced DALL-E, OpenAI's leading image generative AI capable of producing high-quality images from prompts across a wide range of artistic styles. We described the two versions of DALL-E, version 2 and 3, that are currently supported and compared their features. We then generated images using DALL-E 3, highlighting techniques for achieving high-quality results. Following this, we delved into creating edits and variations of existing images, showcasing the capabilities of AI-assisted image editing.

In the next chapter, we will use ChatGPT and DALL-E to build a Next.js web app, showcasing how these tools can aid in generating both code and content for your web development projects.

CHAPTER 5

Building Web Apps with ChatGPT and DALL-E

5.1 Introduction

In this chapter, we'll examine how to use ChatGPT and DALL-E to create web applications with Next.js. Our project will be a company website for a fictional "Magic Carpets Store," aimed at selling and promoting handwoven carpets. The site will include key components: a home page, product pages, an about us section, and a contact page. Using ChatGPT and DALL-E, we will generate designs, before generating the pages with HTML, CSS, JavaScript, and content, showcasing how to write good prompts to achieve the desired design and functionality.

5.2 Setting Up the Project

Before we begin building the website, we need to set up our Next.js project. Next.js is a widely used React framework that offers a well-organized environment for building fast web applications. Its server-side rendering and built-in routing make it a suitable choice for our project.

5.2.1 Installing Prerequisites

Before we proceed with creating our Next.js project, it is essential that the development environment is properly configured. We will need Node.js, a JavaScript environment, which includes a package manager npm (Node Package Manager) to manage and run Next.js commands. Here are the steps to get your system ready on Windows or macOS:

Windows

1. Visit the official Node.js website https://nodejs.org/, and download the latest LTS (Long-Term Support) version of Node.js for Windows. The LTS version is recommended for most users as it provides stability and reliability.

2. Once downloaded, run the installer and follow the prompts. Ensure that you select the option to add Node.js to your system PATH during installation.

macOS

1. Open a terminal (you can find it via Spotlight search or in the Applications ➤ Utilities folder).

2. To install Node.js, you can use Homebrew, a popular package manager for macOS. If you do not have Homebrew installed yet, visit the Homebrew website https://brew.sh/ and follow the instructions provided. The website will give you the command to install Homebrew directly in your terminal.

3. Once Homebrew is installed, install Node.js by running:

   > *brew install node*

CHAPTER 5   BUILDING WEB APPS WITH CHATGPT AND DALL-E

Verifying Node.js Installation

To ensure that Node.js and npm are correctly installed, you can try running the following commands in your terminal:

> *npx --version*

If this returns a version number, you are ready to proceed. If you encounter any issues, you may need to revisit the installation steps or consult the Node.js documentation for troubleshooting tips.

5.2.2 Creating the Next.js App

To create the project, open a terminal and run the following command:

> *npx create-next-app@latest magic-carpets-website*

If it's the first time *create-next-app* has been run on your computer, it will prompt you whether to install Next.js, and you should follow the steps to complete the installation.

You will be prompted with the following questions on how to configure the project. To match the example in this book, answer the questions the same way. If you configure the project differently, you may need to modify the code examples to be compatible:

1. Would you like to use Typescript: **No**/Yes

2. Would you like to use ESLint: **No**/Yes

3. Would you like to use Tailwind CSS: **No**/Yes

4. Would you like to use "src/" directory: No/**Yes**

5. Would you like to use App Router: **No**/Yes

6. Would you like to customize the default import alias: **No**/Yes

CHAPTER 5   BUILDING WEB APPS WITH CHATGPT AND DALL-E

After completing these commands, the project will be set up in a folder called *carpets-website*.

Once the project is created, move into the project directory with:

> *cd magic-carpets-website*

and then install two libraries that we will use in the project: *react-icons* and *yet-another-react-lightbox*:

> *npm install react-icons yet-another-react-lightbox*

Open the *magic-carpets-website* folder in a code editor such as Visual Studio Code. Take a moment to look at the basic file structure of the default Next.js project created as in Figure 5-1.

- The "pages" directory, located in the project root, contains files that represent the different pages in your app, for example, "index.js" contains the code that corresponds to the home page. We will create files in this folder for the pages of our app.

- The "api" directory, located within the pages folder, contains code for functions that run on our web server. For example, "hello.js" contains a function that returns the name "John Doe." We will create functions in the "api" folder that will interact with ChatGPT.

CHAPTER 5   BUILDING WEB APPS WITH CHATGPT AND DALL-E

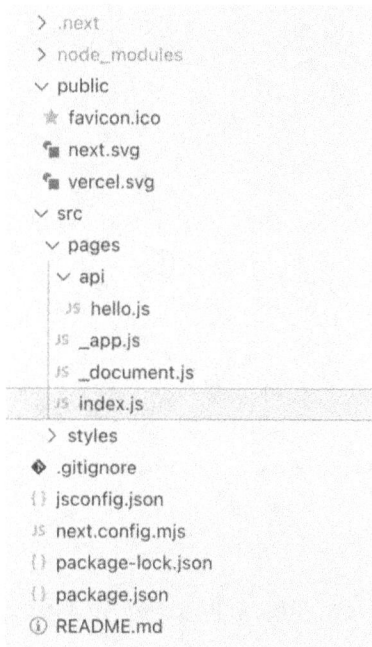

Figure 5-1. *Next.js project structure*

To start the website, run the following command in the terminal:

> *npm run dev*

You will see in the output the URL where the website is running which by default is http://localhost:3000. Open this URL in a web browser to see the default template that is created as shown in Figure 5-2.

Figure 5-2. *The default website created by Next.js*

When you make changes to the code inside the project, the app will automatically refresh and show the changes. To stop running the application, go back to the terminal and press Ctrl+C.

5.2.3 Cleaning the Project Template

Before we start adding our own code, let's delete some of the template code that we don't need so that it doesn't interfere with our project:

1. First, **delete** the following files:
    - src/styles/globals.css
    - src/styles/Home.module.css
    - src/pages/api/hello.js
    - public/next.svg
    - public/vercel.svg

2. Then, open "src/pages/index.js" and delete all the content so it is a blank file.

3. Finally, open "src/pages/_app.js" and **delete** the first line *import "@/styles/globals.css";*.

With our Next.js project set up, we're ready to move on to the next step: generating the user interface. In the next section, we will begin building the interface and functionality of this app with ChatGPT.

5.3 Building the Home Page

The first step in building the home page is to create a basic design that outlines the layout and components. For our needs, a simple sketch will suffice, rather than professional mock-ups or wireframes. We'll use ChatGPT to generate several home page designs, presenting them as ASCII diagrams. Start by opening ChatGPT, create a new chat, and then paste the prompt from Listing 5-1.

Listing 5-1. Prompt to generate wireframe layouts for the home page

```
I'm building a website with React.js with Next.js. Create
a wireframe design for the home page of my company website
called "Magic Carpets" that sells hand woven carpets. Give me
3 different designs that are modern. I want to see the overall
layout of the page and the components in each of them. Present
each wireframe to me visually using ascii art.
```

In the output, you should receive three ASCII diagrams showing a potential layout for the home page. An example of a minimal design is shown in Figure 5-3.

```
+------------------------------------------------------------------+
|                         Navigation Bar                           |
|----------------------------------------------------------------- |
| Home | Products | Contact                                        |
+------------------------------------------------------------------+
|                                                                  |
|                         Hero Section                             |
|                   [Beautiful Hand-Woven Carpets]                 |
|                       [Shop Now Button]                          |
|                                                                  |
+------------------------------------------------------------------+
|                         Product Features                         |
|----------------------------------------------------------------- |
| [Product 1 Image]        | [Product 2 Image]                     |
| [Product 1 Title]        | [Product 2 Title]                     |
| [Product 1 Description]  | [Product 2 Description]               |
| [View Product Button]    | [View Product Button]                 |
+------------------------------------------------------------------+
|                      Customer Testimonials                       |
|----------------------------------------------------------------- |
| "These carpets transformed our home! Absolutely stunning and high quality." |
| - Customer Name                                                  |
|                                                                  |
| "The craftsmanship is incredible. A true piece of art."          |
| - Customer Name                                                  |
+------------------------------------------------------------------+
|                             Footer                               |
|----------------------------------------------------------------- |
| Links: Home | Products | Contact                                 |
| Social Media: [Facebook Icon] [Twitter Icon] [Instagram Icon]    |
+------------------------------------------------------------------+
```

Figure 5-3. *Example ASCII-generated layout for the home page*

If you wish to see more designs, follow up with another prompt requesting more:

`Give me 5 more designs.`

Iterate with ChatGPT over the designs, suggesting the elements you prefer more or the ones you would like to remove.

The next step is to generate the HTML and CSS code. We'll use the design from Listing 5-2 as the template for the page and ask ChatGPT to write the skeleton code. The template can be located in the source code

CHAPTER 5   BUILDING WEB APPS WITH CHATGPT AND DALL-E

for the book in the file *magic-carpets-website/hompage_template.txt*. The source code for this book is available on GitHub via the book's product page, located at www.apress.com/9798868808845.

To generate the code, open a new chat in ChatGPT and enter the prompt in Listing 5-2, pasting the template below the prompt.

Listing 5-2. Prompt to generate HTML and CSS for the page following the layout

```
I'm using React.js with Next.js. Write the page for me with
a layout corresponding to the design below. I will add the
content later. Output any CSS styles using the styled-jsx tag.
Output all the code as a single file.
<paste layout template here>
```

This prompt begins by specifying the frameworks and technologies we're using, ensuring that ChatGPT generates code compatible with our application. It then describes the task of generating code based on the created layout, without including any actual content. Additionally, it instructs ChatGPT to output CSS using the styled-jsx tag, which is the recommended approach for styling individual components in Next.js. By keeping the styles within the same component, it simplifies the process of using ChatGPT to generate code, as we only need to deal with a single file. This way, we can quickly copy and paste the code into our project, avoiding the complexity of managing multiple files.

Once the code has been generated, copy it and paste it into *src/pages/index.js*. To view the result, open a terminal in the *magic-carpets-website* folder and run the command *npm run dev*. Then, open a web browser and go to http://localhost:3000. An example is shown in Figure 5-4. Since ChatGPT often generates different code, your web page may look different, but the core components should be the same. You can regenerate the page multiple times to see different versions. Although they won't be perfectly styled, some generated pages will be of higher quality than others.

CHAPTER 5 BUILDING WEB APPS WITH CHATGPT AND DALL-E

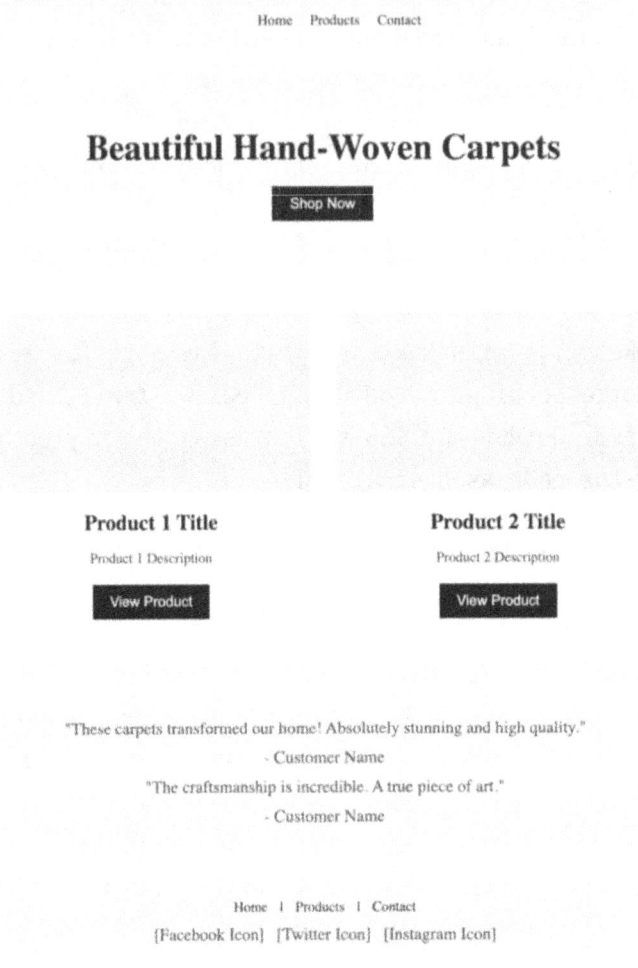

Figure 5-4. *An example basic home page generated from the minimal design*

The color scheme and styles of this page are very basic. Let's add some style and color by getting ChatGPT to generate some CSS styles. Start by copying all the code in *src/pages/index.js*. Then, open a new chat in ChatGPT and enter the prompt from Listing 5-3, pasting the code for the page below it:

Listing 5-3. Adding CSS styles to the home page

```
Modify the CSS for this page to change the following styles:
1. Use a modern font such as Roboto.
2. Colour the buttons with a suitable blue.
3. Use rounded corners everywhere.
4. Have a hover effect on the buttons and links.
<paste code here>
```

The generated page should have a more colorful and friendly appearance such as the example shown in Figure 5-5.

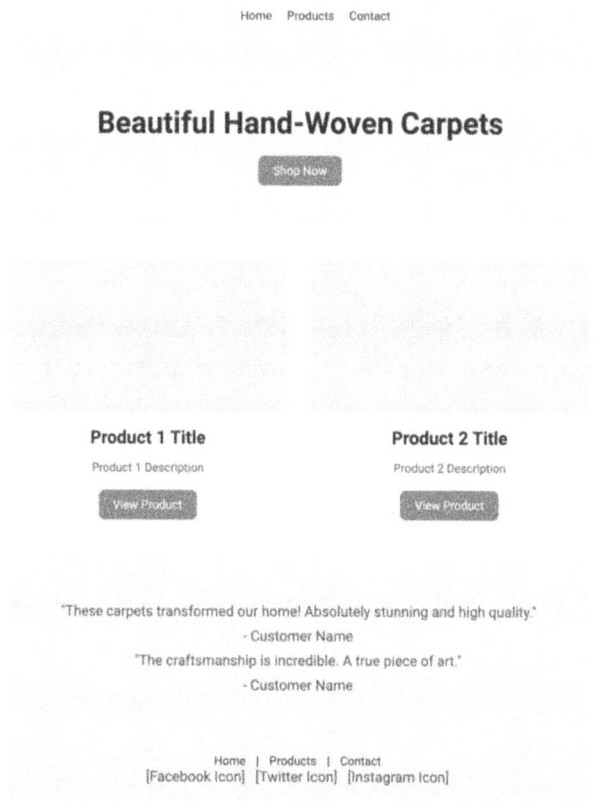

Figure 5-5. CSS styles applied to the home page

CHAPTER 5   BUILDING WEB APPS WITH CHATGPT AND DALL-E

Our home page is progressing, but it is lacking visual elements. Let's use DALL-E to generate a carpet design for the hero section background. Open a new chat with DALL-E and run the prompt in Listing 5-4.

Listing 5-4. Prompt to generate an image of an Armenian carpet

```
An Armenian carpet with light colours and traditional design,
wide aspect ratio.
```

Download the generated image, and save it to *src/public/images/hero.webp*, creating the images folder if it doesn't already exist. To add the image to our page, either modify the code manually, setting the *background-image* CSS style on the hero element, or by using ChatGPT to modify the code in a new chat, using the prompt in Listing 5-5. The result is shown in Figure 5-6.

Listing 5-5. Prompt to modify the background image of the hero section

```
Modify the CSS for the background image of the hero section of
this page to use an image located in "/images/hero.webp". Make
the image cover the whole hero component. Modify the code and
give me the whole file.
```

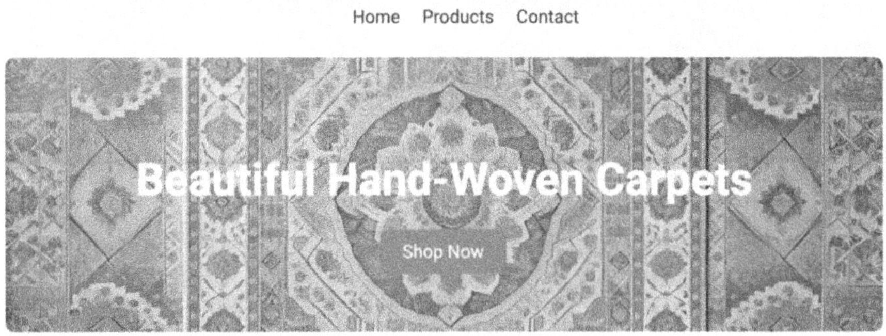

Figure 5-6. *Hero section with the background image from DALL-E*

The text on top of the image is hard to read as it blends into the background. Let's fix that by adding a semitransparent background to text. Open a new chat in ChatGPT and run the prompt in Listing 5-6, pasting in the code for the page below it.

Listing 5-6. Prompt to adjust the text style on the hero image

```
Add a semi-transparent background to the text over the hero
image which stretches the whole width to make it stand
out better.
<paste code here>
```

The result now looks as in Figure 5-7.

Figure 5-7. *Improving the readability of text over the hero image*

Our page also needs product images. To address this, use the same prompt from Listing 5-4 to generate two more carpet pictures. Save these images as *product1.webp* and *product2.webp* in the *src/images* folder. After that, you can either manually update the CSS to point to these images, or open a new chat in ChatGPT and run the prompt in Listing 5-7, pasting in the code from the page below the prompt. This will automatically update the code to include the new product images.

75

Listing 5-7. Prompt to update the two product images

```
Modify the CSS for the background image for the two product
images on this page to use the two images "/images/product1.
webp" and "/images/product2.webp". Make the image cover the
existing area.
<paste code here>
```

Additionally, update the text for the products, either with your own text or using ChatGPT to generate some for you with the following prompt:

```
Give me two short product descriptions around two sentences for
an Armenian carpet, together with product names.
```

The product section should now look similar to Figure 5-8.

Harmony Carpet

The Elegance Armenian Carpet features a stunning blend of geometric motifs and floral patterns, hand-knotted with premium wool. Its deep, earthy tones and exceptional detail offer both luxury and a connection to Armenia's rich cultural tapestry

View Product

Elegance Carpet

The Elegance Armenian Rug features a stunning blend of geometric motifs and floral patterns, hand-knotted with premium wool. Its deep, earthy tones and exceptional detail offer both luxury and a connection to Armenia's rich cultural tapestry

View Product

Figure 5-8. *Updated product section*

The testimonial section of our page needs a style boost. We can enhance it by creating an animated testimonial component, where the testimonials change every few seconds. In a new chat, enter the prompt in Listing 5-8, pasting in all the code from the home page below.

Listing 5-8. Prompt to update the testimonial section to be animated

```
Update the testimonial section on this page, written with
React.js using Next.js, to be a testimonial slider with the
customer quotes shown with a handwriting font. Output all the
code as a single file.
<paste code here>
```

Copy the new code into *index.js* and view it to see the changes. Our home page is almost ready. Now, let's enhance the social media links at the bottom by replacing them with icons from the *react-icons* library. Copy the current code from your page, then open a new chat in ChatGPT, and enter the prompt from Listing 5-9, pasting your code below it.

Listing 5-9. Prompt to update the social media icons

```
Update the social media links in the footer of this page,
written with React.js using Next.js, to use icons from the
react-icons library. Output all the code in a single file.
<past code here>
```

After applying the new code from ChatGPT, the home page should now look similar to Figure 5-9.

CHAPTER 5   BUILDING WEB APPS WITH CHATGPT AND DALL-E

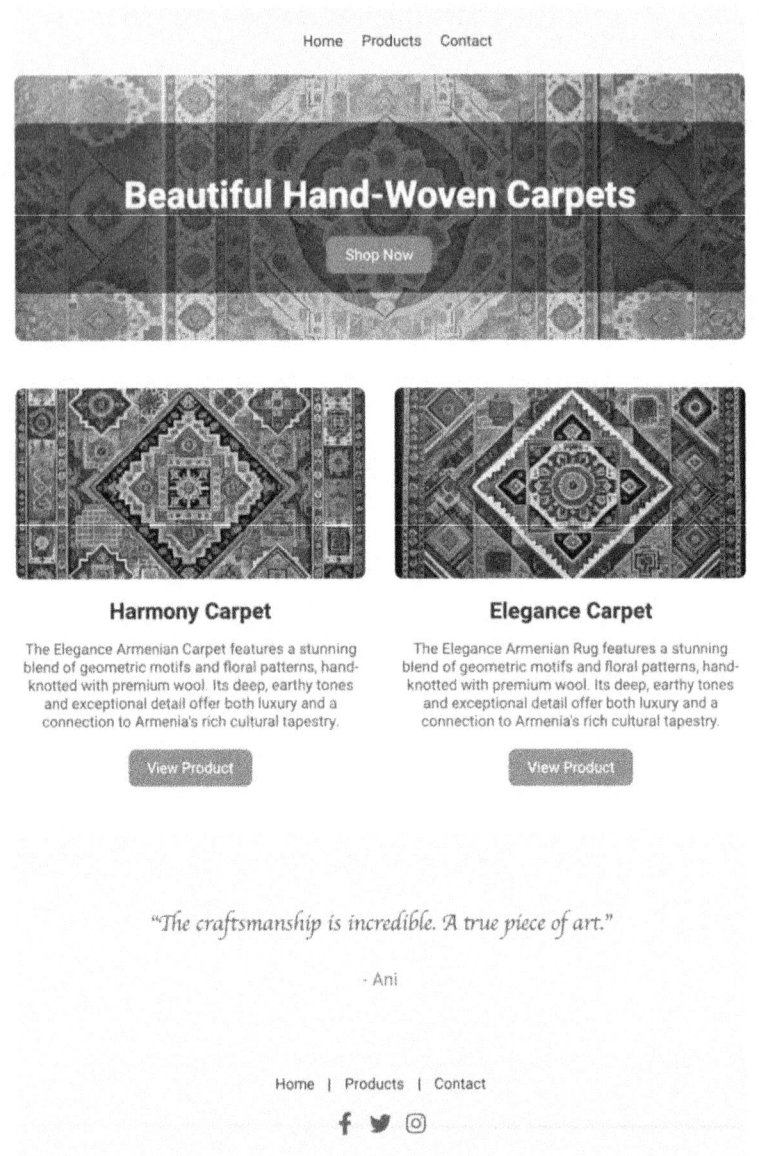

Figure 5-9. Completed design of the carpets' website home page

This completes our home page. In the next section, we will implement the product pages.

5.4 Building the Product Pages

To build the product pages, we'll get ChatGPT to generate them following the design and layout of the home page. The product page should feature an image of the carpet which when clicked opens in a lightbox viewer. Beside the image, there should be the description of the carpet, along with a price and a "Buy" button. Beneath this, a table should display the specifications of the carpet. To begin, copy the code from *src/pages/index.js*, then open a new chat in ChatGPT, and enter the prompt in Listing 5-10, pasting the code below the prompt.

Listing 5-10. Prompt to generate a product page for the first carpet

```
I'm building a web app with React.js using Next.js. Build a
product page for the first product from this homepage that
follows the same styles, and uses the same image. Include the
following elements on the product page:
1. A photo of the carpet. When the photo is clicked it should
   enlarge to fill the page using a lightbox using yet-another-
   react-lightbox.
2. The description.
3. The price located to the right of the image in bold.
4. A "Buy" button.
5. A table with the following row headers: material, size, weight.
Remember to import the 'react-icons/fa'.
Output all the code as a single file.
<paste code here>
```

To ensure ChatGPT incorporates all the features, we write them as a numbered list. When running this prompt, we often found that ChatGPT forgot to import the *react-icons* library to display the social media icons. To prevent this, we specifically include the instruction: "Remember to import the 'react-icons/fa'".

CHAPTER 5   BUILDING WEB APPS WITH CHATGPT AND DALL-E

Once the code is generated, copy it and paste it into a new file called *src/pages/product1.js*. Then, open your web browser, and go to `https://localhost:3000/product1` to view the result. An example is shown in Figure 5-10. Try clicking the image and verify that it opens into the full page using the lightbox. To adjust any details in the description or table, edit the relevant text in the code.

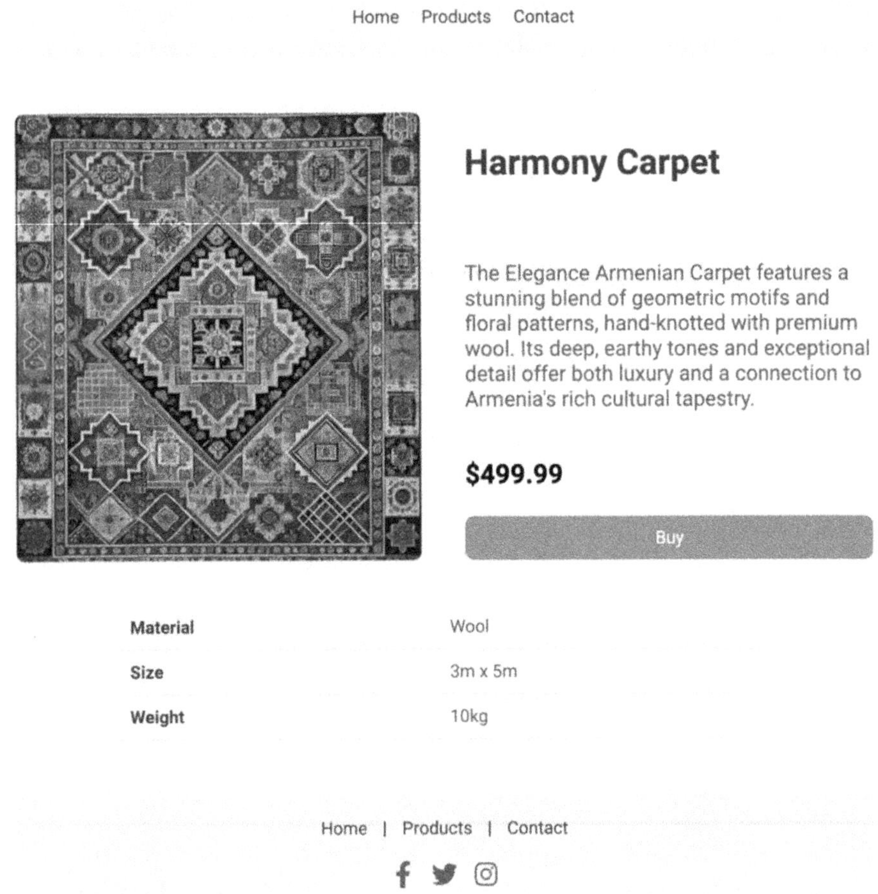

Figure 5-10. *Product page generated for the first product*

CHAPTER 5   BUILDING WEB APPS WITH CHATGPT AND DALL-E

We can easily repeat this process to generate a page for the second product. Enter and run the following prompt in the same chat in ChatGPT:

```
Do this again but with the second product from the homepage.
```

Copy the generated code, and paste it into a new file called *src/pages/product2.js*. Then, in your web browser, navigate to https://localhost:3000/product2 to verify it is the same page but with the details of the second product.

Now that we've created two individual product pages, the next step is to generate a list page for viewing all the products. To do this, in the same chat in ChatGPT that we generated the two product pages, enter and run the prompt in Listing 5-11.

Listing 5-11. Prompt to generate a product list page

```
Now generate a product list page that lists both products with
their image and title.
The title and image should be a link that navigates to either
"/product1.js" or "/product2.js".
The page should have a heading "Products".
When using next/link do not use an 'a' tag inside it.
```

In Next.js, the "Link" component previously required an "a" tag inside it, but in the latest version, this causes an error. To ensure ChatGPT generates code with the correct, updated syntax, we add a reminder not to insert "a" tags within the "Link" component when creating links to navigate to the product pages.

Once the code is generated, copy it and paste it into a new file called *src/pages/list.js*. In your browser, navigate to https://localhost:3000/list to see the final result. An example is shown in Figure 5-11.

Figure 5-11. Example of the product list page

To finish the pages, update the hyperlinks in *index.js*, *product1.js*, *product2.js*, and *list.js* so that the "View Product" pages link to the */product1* and */product2* pages and the "Shop Now" button and the "Products" links go to the */list* page.

This completes the implementation of the product pages. In the next section, we will generate a contact page.

5.5 Building the Contact Page

To demonstrate how to create forms, we'll build a contact page containing a form with three inputs: name, email, and message. Below the form, there will be a "Send" button. For now, we will only implement the UI of this page, as sending an actual message would require integrating with an email or messaging service.

We will create the contact page similarly to how we created the product pages using the home page as a template. Begin by copying the code in *src/pages/index.js*. Then in ChatGPT, open a new chat and enter the prompt in Listing 5-12, pasting the code for the page below it.

Listing 5-12. Prompt to generate the contact page

```
I'm building a web app with React.js using Next.js. Build a
Contact page based on this homepage as a template. The contact
page should have the following elements:
1. A page heading with the text "Send us a message"
2. A form to enter name, email address, and message.
3. A "Send" button.
Remember to include the social media links in the footer.
Output all the code as a single file.
<paste code here>
```

As before, we will use a numbered list of requirements to ensure ChatGPT implements all the necessary features for the contact page. The comment "remember to include the social media links in the footer" was necessary, as this is for ChatGPT to include them in the generated code; otherwise, ChatGPT occasionally decided to remove them from the home page template when generating the new code.

Once you have the generated code, copy it and paste it in a new file *src/pages/contact.js*. Then, in a browser, navigate to http://localhost:3000/contact. The page should look similar to Figure 5-12.

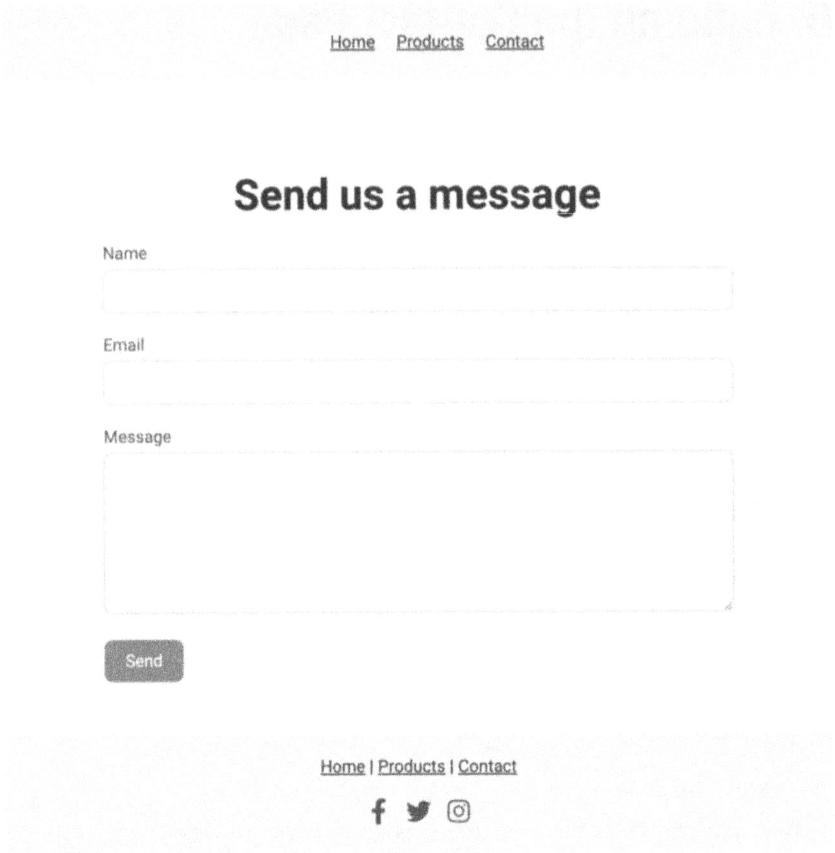

Figure 5-12. The generated contact page

To complete the implementation, update the links to the contact page in the headers and footers of the other pages. This completes the implementation of the site.

5.6 Summary

In this chapter, we built a website from scratch using ChatGPT to generate the code. We began by creating an ASCII diagram to design the home page layout. Next, we generated the page's basic structure, followed by the CSS

CHAPTER 5   BUILDING WEB APPS WITH CHATGPT AND DALL-E

styles, and incorporated text and images produced with ChatGPT and DALL-E. This process demonstrated the workflow for how to effectively build pages by writing prompts with multiple numbered steps to guide ChatGPT through the required changes.

ChatGPT enabled us to generate the code and content for this website significantly faster than we could have done writing everything manually. The key to becoming proficient at coding with ChatGPT is consistent practice and experimentation. This helps you understand its strengths and limitations, as well as how to craft effective prompts to make the most of its capabilities.

In the next chapter, we will shift our focus to the OpenAI APIs, exploring how to integrate generative AI into web applications.

CHAPTER 6

Overview of the OpenAI APIs

6.1 Introduction

So far, we have explored two of OpenAI's flagship AI tools: ChatGPT and DALL-E. Both of these tools can be accessed via a web interface that resembles a chat application. But what if we want to integrate chat and image generation in our own web applications? Fortunately, OpenAI offers this capability through an Application Programming Interface (API). In this chapter, we will introduce the OpenAI APIs, explain how they work, and how to set them up. We will then demonstrate how to use the OpenAI APIs in practice by creating a Next.js web app using OpenAI Node.js library to interact with the chat and image generation APIs.

6.2 What Are the OpenAI APIs?

An Application Programming Interface (API) is a collection of functions and standards that allow different software applications to communicate and work together. They allow you to incorporate functionality provided by external services into your own applications.

CHAPTER 6   OVERVIEW OF THE OPENAI APIS

OpenAI provides several APIs to utilize their generative AI capabilities including

1. **Chat API:** This API uses models including GPT-4o and GPT-4o mini to generate text or have chat conversations like in the ChatGPT interface.

2. **Image API:** This API uses models like DALL-E 2 and DALL-E 3 to generate images from a prompt. It also supports generating edits and variations of a given image.

3. **Fine-Tuning API:** These APIs can be used to fine-tune the responses and behavior of GPT models based on a given dataset.

4. **Embeddings API:** These APIs can be used to get GPT to query for information in an external dataset it was not trained on and provide the results in its responses.

5. **Audio API:** This API turns input text into audio using OpenAI's text-to-speech models.

In this chapter, we will focus on the Chat API and Image API, as these are the ones we will use throughout the rest of this book. If you wish to explore the other APIs and review the latest features, you can do so by referring to the OpenAI API Reference.[1]

6.3 Pricing and Usage

OpenAI uses a tiered pricing structure for their APIs. However, unlike ChatGPT subscriptions where there are tiers offering varying message

---

[1] https://platform.openai.com/docs/api-reference/

limits and features, the APIs are charged by usage. Every API has a fixed cost determined by the model you are using and the amount of data transferred. In this section, we will break down how these costs are calculated. It's important to pay attention to your API costs and expenses when developing and testing your applications. While the advertised prices may look small, they can accumulate rapidly, particularly if your app has significant usage. When estimating your own costs, make sure to review the latest prices on the OpenAI platform website.[2]

6.3.1 Chat API Pricing

In Chapter 3 Section 3.4.1, we described how LLMs such as ChatGPT process text in *tokens* – chunks of text that range from a single character to several characters long. The cost of using the Chat APIs is determined by the number of input tokens (the prompt) and the number of output tokens (the response). The more tokens used, the more expensive the interaction. Typically, input and output tokens are priced differently, with output tokens being several times more expensive. Table 6-1 summarizes the costs of the GPT-4 era models as of August 2024. On OpenAI's pricing page, costs are generally listed per 1 million tokens. To make the pricing clearer and easier, we've calculated the approximate price per 1,000 English words, which equates to roughly 1,330 tokens.

---

[2] https://openai.com/api/pricing/

Table 6-1. Pricing of the Chat API endpoints for each GPT model as of August 2024

Model	Input Token Price per 1 Million Tokens	Approximate Price per 1000 English Words	Output Token Price per 1 Million Tokens	Approximate Price per 1000 English Words
GPT-4o	$5.00	~ $0.007	$15.00	~ $0.02
GPT-4o mini	$0.15	~ $0.0002	$0.6	~ $0.0008
GPT-4-turbo (Legacy GPT-4)	$10	~ $0.014	$30	~ $0.04

The price differences between the models are substantial. For instance, the cost of using GPT-4o mini is *33 times* cheaper than GPT-4o, while the legacy GPT-4 model costs twice as much as GPT-4o. When developing and testing your applications with the Chat API, it would be wise to test whether the performance of GPT-4o mini is adequate for your needs, as the cost savings could be significant. Historically, each new release of GPT-4 models has brought about a reduction in API costs, and as LLMs become more efficient to run, prices are likely to continue decreasing.

6.3.2 Image API Pricing

The Image APIs are priced according to the version of DALL-E you are using and the size and quality of the generated image. Unlike the Chat APIs, there is no cost associated with the number of tokens in the prompt used to generate the image. Table 6-2 summarizes the costs of the Image APIs as of August 2024.

Table 6-2. *Pricing of the Image API endpoints as of August 2024*

Model	Image Quality	Image Resolution	Price per Image
DALL-E 3	Standard	1024×1024	$0.04
	Standard	1024×1792, 1792×1024	$0.08
	HD	1024×1024	$0.08
	HD	1024×1792, 1792×1024	$0.12
DALL-E 2	Standard	1024×1024	$0.02
	Standard	512×512	$0.018
	Standard	256×256	$0.016

The cost of generating images with DALL-E 3 is significantly higher, with a standard quality 1024×1024 image costing twice as much as the same image generated with DALL-E 2. If your application only requires smaller, standard quality images, DALL-E 2 might suffice, resulting in significant cost savings.

6.3.3 Pricing of Other OpenAI APIs

In this book, we will solely focus on the Image and Chat APIs, so we will not delve into the costs of the audio, fine-tuning, and embedding APIs. For the latest costs of these APIs, refer to OpenAI's API pricing page.[3]

6.3.4 Batch Pricing

In April 2024, OpenAI introduced *Batch Pricing* for situations where the results of the API calls are not needed immediately. It is available for chat-based models including GPT-4o and GPT-4o mini, as well as for the

---

[3] https://openai.com/api/pricing/

text embedding APIs. Requests made via the *Batch API* are processed within a 24-hour window and have a 50% discount. The requests are executed when OpenAI's systems have lower demand, meaning results can be returned at any point during that 24-hour period. If your application does not require instant results, this can lead to significant cost savings. For more information on batch processing, refer to the documentation on OpenAI's website.[4]

6.3.5 Pay-As-You-Go with Credits

OpenAI uses a pay-as-you-go model, meaning you only pay for the resources you actually use. However, unlike many cloud platforms, you must pay for your API usage upfront by purchasing credits. Every time you use the APIs, the cost is deducted from your available credits. If your credits reach zero, then your API requests will fail, resulting in errors until you replenish your credits. In Section 6.4, we will discuss how to create an account and add credits in the OpenAI API platform.

6.3.6 Usage Limits

To prevent misuse and ensure fair access, OpenAI sets *usage limits* on each API. These allowances are organized into tiers starting from Free, Tier 1, up to Tier 5. Each tier has a qualification criteria and maximum credit spend, based on the number of credits you have paid to your account and the number of days since your first successful payment. The qualification criteria and usage limits for the first three tiers, as of August 2024, are displayed in Table 6-3. For the latest information and details on the higher usage tiers, consult the OpenAI documentation.[5]

---

[4]https://platform.openai.com/docs/guides/batch/overview
[5]https://platform.openai.com/docs/guides/rate-limits/usage-tiers

Table 6-3. *OpenAI usage tier qualification and credit usage limits as of August 2024*

Tier	Qualification	Credit Usage Limits
Free	User must be in an allowed geography	$100 USD/month
Tier 1	$5 USD paid to your account	$100 USD/month
Tier 2	$50 USD paid to your account	$500 USD/month

In addition to credit usage limits, OpenAI also enforces *rate limits that* restrict how frequently each model can be used, though not how frequently each API is accessed. For example, if you reach the maximum allowance for GPT-4o mini using the Chat API, you can still use the Chat API with GPT-4o, provided you haven't hit the maximum allowance for that model.

Rate limits are applied to models in the following three ways:

- **Rate Per Minute (RPM):** Defines the maximum number of requests you can make to a model each minute

- **Rate Per Day (RPD):** Defines the maximum number of requests you can make to a model each day

- **Tokens Per Minute (TPM):** Defines the maximum number of tokens you can send to a model each minute

Table 6-4 displays the Tier 1 rate limits for chat and image models as of August 2024. For the latest information and the details on the higher usage tiers, consult the OpenAI documentation.[6]

---

[6] https://platform.openai.com/docs/guides/rate-limits/usage-tiers

Table 6-4. *Tier 1 rate limits for chat and image generation models as of August 2024*

Model	RPM	RPD	TPM
GPT-4o	500	None	30,000
GPT-4o mini	500	10,000	200,000
GPT-4-turbo	500	None	30,000
DALL-E-2	5 images/minute	None	None
DALL-E-3	5 images/minute	None	None

For hobby projects and experimentation, these limits are unlikely to be an issue. However, if you're developing a product for commercial release, you should familiarize yourself with OpenAI's latest pricing details and usage limits to avoid any restrictions that may be placed on your application.

Having covered the APIs that OpenAI offers, along with the associated costs and usage limitations, we will now move on to setting up an API account and learning how to use the APIs.

6.4 Creating an API Account and API Key

When you sign up to ChatGPT, the account you create also provides access to OpenAI's API platform. The platform organizes your API usage into *Organizations* and *Projects*. By default, your account includes a *Personal* organization and a *Default project*. Each project allows you to manage and review the API usage of a single application, while multiple applications can be managed under a single organization.

CHAPTER 6 OVERVIEW OF THE OPENAI APIS

6.4.1 Creating an API Account

In this book, we will be developing web applications that use the OpenAI APIs. Let's set up a project for them in our OpenAI platform by following these steps:

1. **Log In:** Log in to the OpenAI API platform using your ChatGPT account credentials: `https://platform.openai.com/`.

2. **Create Project:** From the OpenAI API platform home page, click "Default project" in the top left drop-down followed by "Create project," as in Figure 6-1.

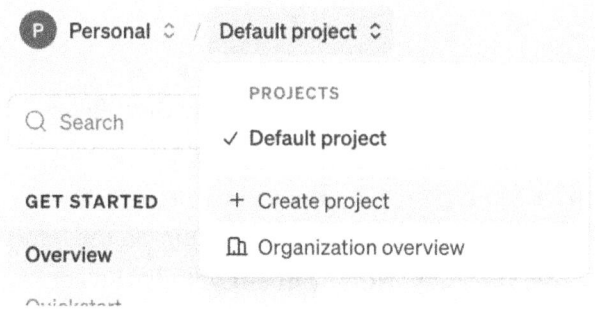

Figure 6-1. *Creating a new project in the OpenAI API platform*

Enter a name for the project, for example, "genai-web-dev", and then, click "Create," as in Figure 6-2.

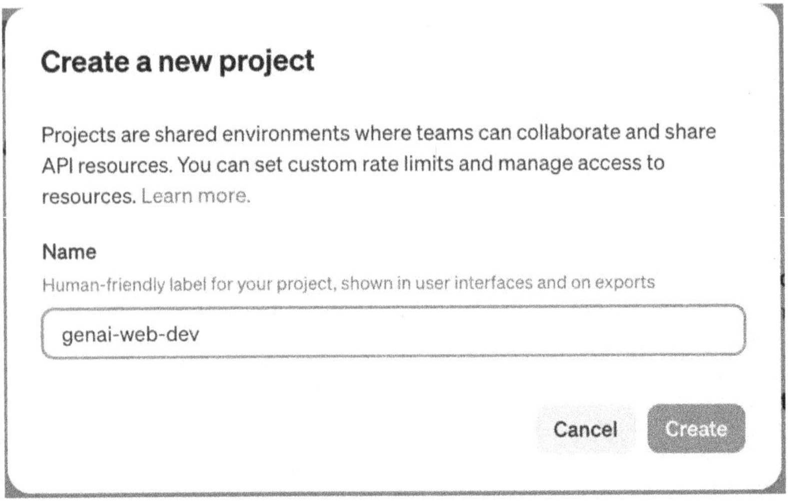

Create a new project

Projects are shared environments where teams can collaborate and share API resources. You can set custom rate limits and manage access to resources. Learn more.

Name
Human-friendly label for your project, shown in user interfaces and on exports

    genai-web-dev

Cancel   Create

Figure 6-2. Naming and creating a new project in the OpenAI API platform

3. **Add Payment Details:** In order to use the APIs, we must add some credits. Following the steps illustrated in Figure 6-3, click the cog icon in the top right of the page, and then, in the menu on the left, click "Billing" then "Add payment details." Select "I am an individual" and enter your card details as prompted.

CHAPTER 6   OVERVIEW OF THE OPENAI APIS

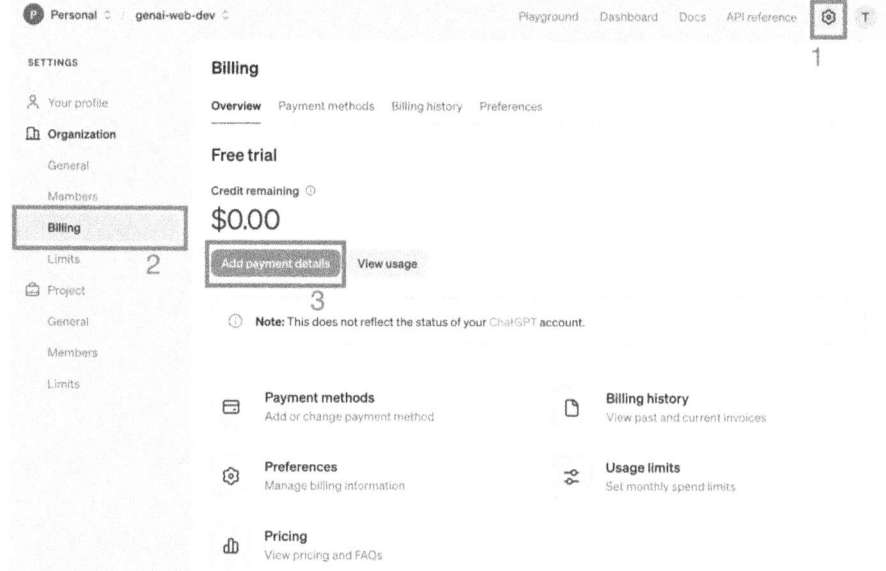

Figure 6-3. *Adding payment details to an OpenAI API account*

4. **Add Credits:** To use the APIs, we must pay for some credits. The minimum credit amount is $5 USD, and this will be sufficient for the projects in this book. To add credits, click "Add to credit balance," enter $5, select your payment method, and click continue to fund your account (see Figure 6-4).

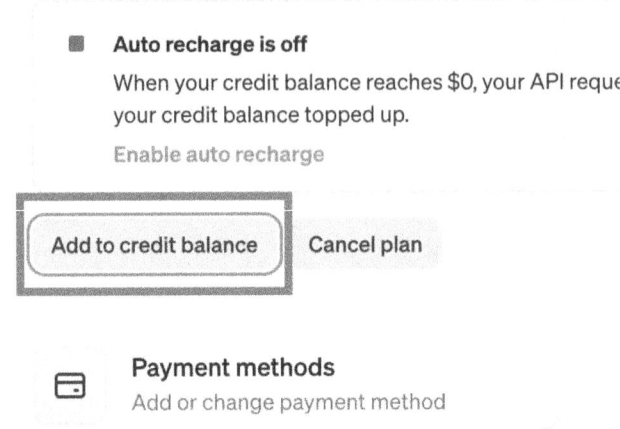

Figure 6-4. *Adding credits to a project*

This completes all the steps required to create and set up our API project account.

6.4.2 Creating an API Key

Before you can use the OpenAI APIs from your applications, you'll need an API key. This is a unique identifier for authenticating your requests and granting access to the APIs on the platform. You can create an API key by following these steps:

1. **Go to the API Keys Page:** In the API platform, click "Dashboard" in the menu in the top right, followed by "API keys" in the left-hand menu, and then click "Create API Key" as shown in Figure 6-5.

CHAPTER 6   OVERVIEW OF THE OPENAI APIS

Figure 6-5.   Navigating to create a new API key

2. **Create API Key:** In the dialog that appears, enter a name for the API key, and click "Create secret key" (see Figure 6-6).

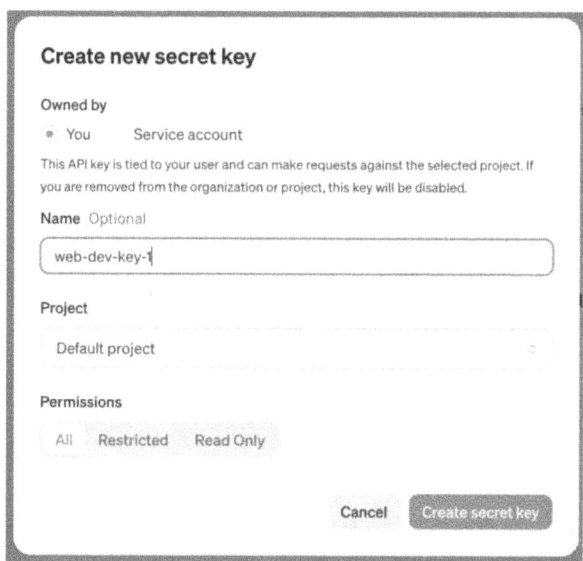

Figure 6-6.   Creating a new API key

3. **Copy and Securely Store the Key:** Copy the key that is generated, and store it in a secure location such as a password manager (see Figure 6-7). Your API key is sensitive information and should be treated with the same level of care as a password. This is the only opportunity you will have to view and copy the API key within the OpenAI platform. If you don't save the key, then you will need to delete it and create a new one.

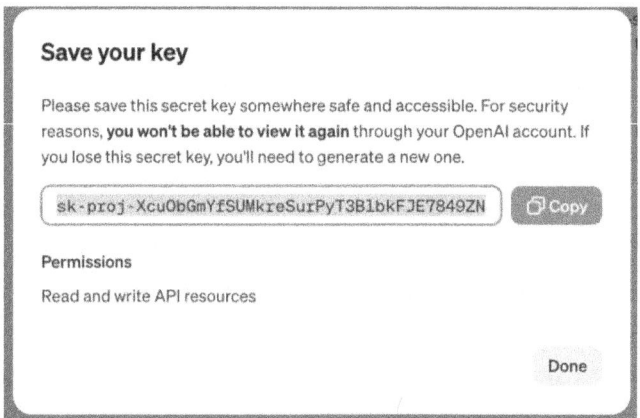

Figure 6-7. Copying and saving the API key

This completes the steps for generating and saving an API key for your project.

6.4.3 Keeping Your API Key Secure

Your API key is sensitive information which grants access to OpenAI APIs through your account. If another person obtains your API key, they can use the APIs, with the associated costs being charged to your account. To ensure your API key remains secure, you should follow these best practices:

1. **Store API Keys Securely:** Only store your API key in secure locations such as a password manager or other encrypted storage. When developing web applications on your computer, provide the key through an environment variable or other secure storage. See Section 6.6.3 for how to do this in Next.js.

2. **Do Not Commit Keys to Git:** Never commit your API keys into git or any version control system because if your repository is published or shared, your key could be exposed to others. If you accidentally commit the key, delete it from the OpenAI API platform and generate a new one. Simply deleting the key from the file and making another commit isn't enough, because the key will still exist in the git history and remain accessible to others.

3. **Rotate Keys Periodically:** As a security best practice, periodically generate new API keys and replace the old ones, for instance, every year. This reduces the risk of accidentally leaked keys being exploited by others.

By following these practices, you can help protect your API key and avoid unwanted usage and charges.

In the next section, we will explore the OpenAI APIs by experimenting with the Playground interface. This will give us a practical understanding of how the APIs function and allow us to test various features before integrating them into our web applications.

6.5 Experimenting with the API Playground

The OpenAI Playground is a web-based interface where you can experiment with OpenAI APIs without needing to write any code. It's a convenient interface for testing and comparing outputs with different models and parameters. As of August 2024, only the Chat API and text-to-speech APIs are available through the Playground. To access it, click "Playground" in the top-right menu of the OpenAI platform.

When the Playground opens, you'll be directed to the chat page for exploring the Chat APIs. See Figure 6-8 for a description of the elements on this page. In the top-left corner, there is a dropdown menu for selecting the GPT model. Below that is a text box for entering the *system prompt*, which customizes how the GPT will respond to subsequent messages (see Chapter 3 Section 3.4.2). To the right, there is a panel for adjusting the model parameters, allowing you to fine-tune how the model behaves. At the bottom of the page is a text box for entering prompts.

CHAPTER 6   OVERVIEW OF THE OPENAI APIS

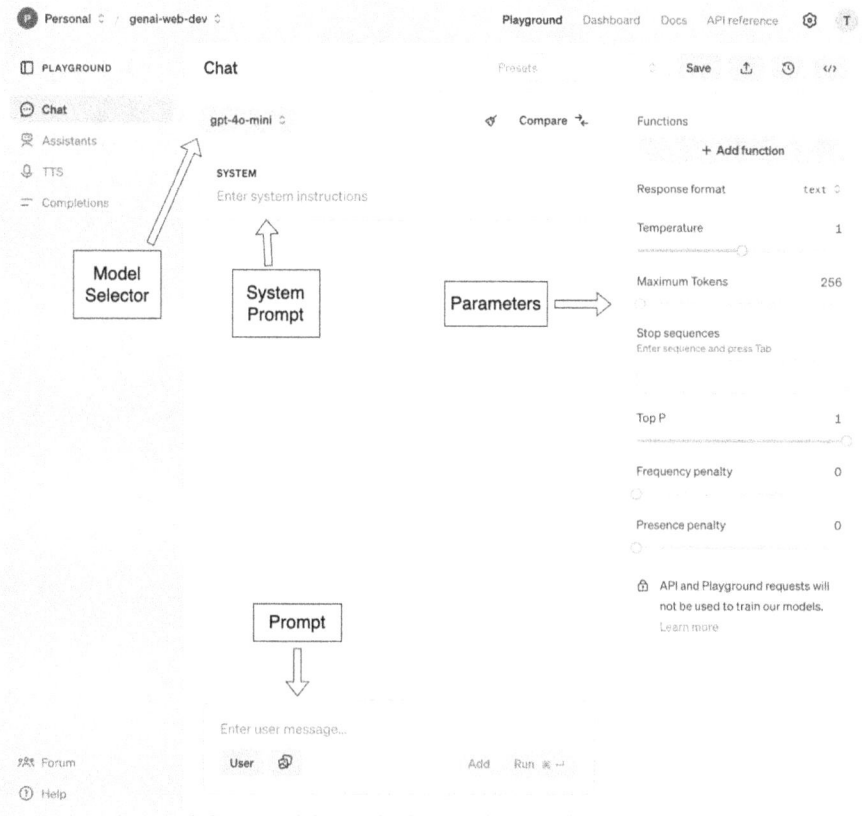

Figure 6-8. *Overview of OpenAI API Playground*

Let's experiment with a practical example. First, in the model selector, choose gpt-4o-mini, and in the system prompt, enter "Respond to all messages using tech and business jargon." Next, in the prompt box at the bottom, write something like "Give me a recipe for borscht," and click "Run." The model should generate a response that starts with a recipe for borscht but incorporates heavy tech and business jargon (see an example in Figure 6-9).

CHAPTER 6   OVERVIEW OF THE OPENAI APIS

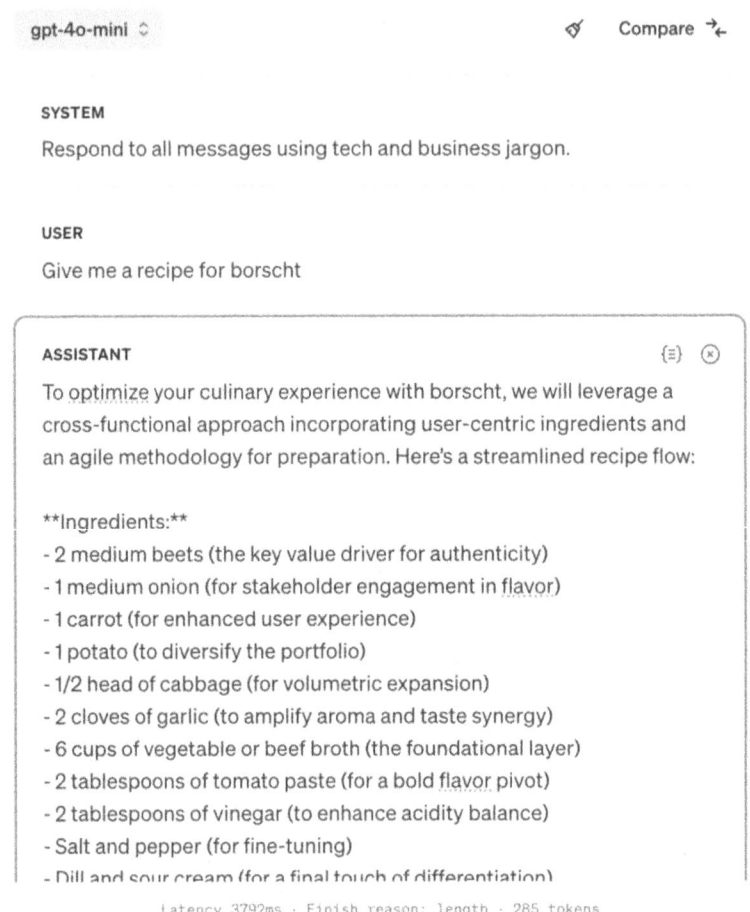

Figure 6-9. Example prompt using the Chat API via the API Playground

6.5.1 Adjusting Parameters

On the right-hand side of the Playground, you'll find controls for adjusting various parameters that influence how the GPT model generates responses. By fine-tuning these settings, you can significantly impact the quality, style, and relevance of the output:

CHAPTER 6   OVERVIEW OF THE OPENAI APIS

- **Temperature:** This parameter controls the randomness of the model and ranges between 0 and 2. A higher temperature (e.g., 1.2) will produce more diverse and unpredictable outputs, while a lower temperature (e.g., 0.8) will result in more deterministic responses.

- **Top P:** Similar to temperature, top P also adjusts randomness by limiting the range of tokens to select from at each prediction step. It takes a value between 0 (pick only the single most likely token) and 1 (pick from all possible tokens). It is recommended to only adjust the Temperature or Top P, not both.

- **Maximum Tokens:** This sets a cap on the length of the generated response, ensuring it doesn't continue indefinitely. Note that this is different to the "context length" which is the maximum amount of text the GPT can process at one time when predicting the next token (see Chapter 3 Section 3.4.1).

- **Frequency Penalty:** This discourages repetition by penalizing tokens based on how frequently they appear in the output so far. It ranges between 0 (no penalty) to 1 (strong penalty for repetition).

- **Presence Penalty:** Similar to Frequency Penalty, this penalizes tokens based on whether they've already appeared in the generated text. It also ranges between 0 (no penalty) to 1 (strong penalty for repeating tokens that have already been used).

As an example, let's experiment with the *temperature* setting to see how it affects the generated output. Start by setting the temperature to 1.2, and run the same "Give me a recipe for borscht" prompt again. If you don't notice much difference in the output, increase the temperature

CHAPTER 6   OVERVIEW OF THE OPENAI APIS

to 1.4 and repeat, raising the temperature in steps of 0.2 each time. See an example in Figure 6-10. As you increase the temperature, the output will become increasingly random until eventually the model returns nonsensical output.

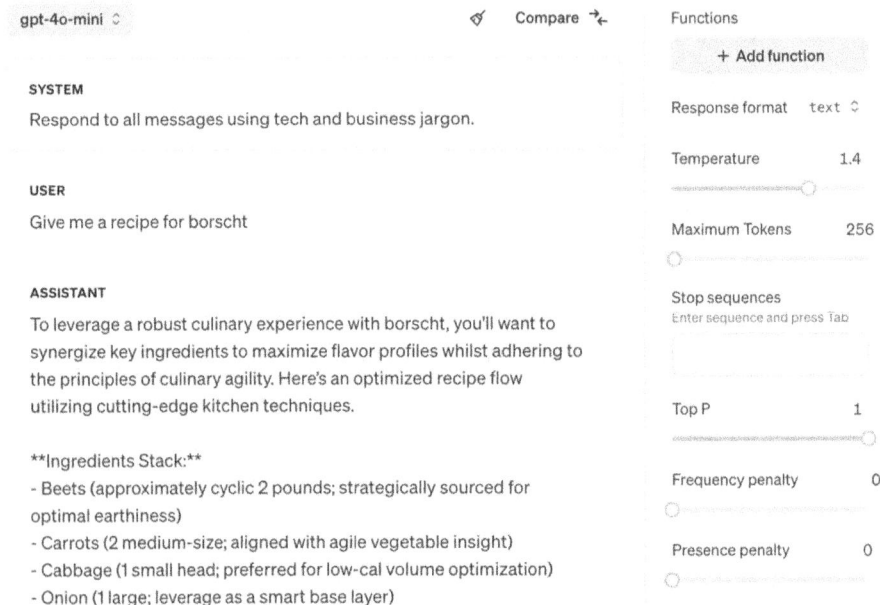

Figure 6-10. Higher temperature results in increasingly random outputs

Next, try decreasing the temperature in steps of 0.2 and running the prompt again. As the temperature decreases toward zero, the prompt becomes more deterministic. For a given low temperature, clear the chat, and repeat the prompt multiple times, observing that similar if not identical output emerges each time.

Experiment with the other parameters, and compare how they alter the generated outputs for different prompts. Don't hesitate to try different combinations and see how they affect the output. As you gain experience, you'll develop a better intuition for which settings work best for different tasks and desired outcomes.

6.6 Using the OpenAI APIs with Next.js

In this section, we will explore how to use the OpenAI APIs within web applications by building a simple web app with Next.js. The app will have a single page with two forms, one for generating text using the Chat API and another for generating images using DALL-E. Each form will have a text box for entering a prompt and a submit button to generate output based on the prompt. The text response or the generated image will then be displayed underneath the forms. The source code for this book is available on GitHub via the book's product page, located at www.apress.com/9798868808845.

6.6.1 Setting Up the Next.js Project

Before setting up the project, ensure you have Node.js LTS installed. Refer to Chapter 5, Section 5.2, for instructions on how to do this.

To create the project, open a terminal and run the following command:

> *npx create-next-app@latest content-generator-app*

You will be prompted with the following questions on how to configure the project. To match the example in this book, answer the questions the same way. If you configure the project differently, you may need to modify the code examples to be compatible:

1. Would you like to use Typescript: **No**/Yes
2. Would you like to use ESLint: **No**/Yes
3. Would you like to use Tailwind CSS: **No**/Yes
4. Would you like to use "src/" directory: No/**Yes**
5. Would you like to use App Router: **No**/Yes
6. Would you like to customize the default import alias: **No**/Yes

After completing these commands, the project will be created in a folder called *content-generator-app*.

Next, in your terminal, change to the project folder by running:

> *cd content-generator-app*

and then install the OpenAI API Node.js library:

> *npm install openai*

Finally, delete the template code that we don't need so that it doesn't interfere with our project:

1. First, **delete** the following files:
   - src/styles/globals.css
   - src/styles/Home.module.css
   - src/pages/api/hello.js
   - public/next.svg
   - public/vercel.svg
2. Then, open "src/pages/index.js" and delete all the content so it is a blank file.
3. Finally, open "src/pages/_app.js" and **delete** the first line *import "@/styles/globals.css";*.

This completes the setup of our project.

6.6.2 Generating the UI

Following the prompting strategies from Chapter 4, let's generate the UI for our page using ChatGPT. Create a new chat, ensure that ChatGPT-4o or 4o-mini is selected, then paste and run the prompt in Listing 6-1.

Listing 6-1. Prompt for generating the content generator UI

```
I'm writing a web page in React using NextJS. The page has two
HTML forms.
The first form collects one text input: "Prompt", and has a
submit button with text "Generate Text". When the submit button
is clicked it calls an API endpoint 'api/generate-text' passing
the input prompt. The API returns a text result in a field
called 'result'. The result text should be displayed underneath
the form.
The second form collects one text input: "Prompt", and has
a submit button with text "Generate Image". When the submit
button is clicked it calls an API endpoint 'api/generate-image'
passing the input prompt. The API returns a text result in a
field called 'result'. The result is an image URL and the image
should be displayed underneath the form.
The submit buttons for both forms will be disabled when either
form is submitted and re-enabled when submission has finished.
Include some CSS styles inline to make it look modern. Output
all of the code as a single file.
```

In Chapters 8–10, we will explain the logic of prompts like this one in greater detail. ChatGPT should generate a single block of code containing all the logic for the UI. If you get more than one block of code, regenerate the prompt or respond with a follow-up prompt "Give me all the code as a single file." Copy the generated code and paste into "src/pages/index.js". Once complete, start your web app from the terminal by running:

> *npm run dev*

Open a web browser and navigate to *https://localhost:3000* where you will see the UI of your site, which should be similar to Figure 6-11.

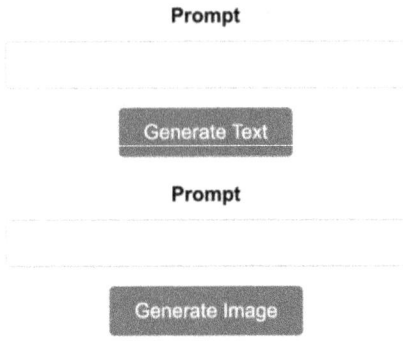

Figure 6-11. *UI for the content generator app*

Currently, the "Generate" buttons don't work as we haven't added the backend code that calls the OpenAI APIs. First, we will add our OpenAI API key to our project and then implement the code for generating content.

6.6.3 Adding an OpenAI API Key

In the "content-generator-app" folder, create a new file called ".env" and add the following text:

OPENAI_API_KEY=sk-xxx

Replacing "sk-xxx" with your generated API key from Section 6.4.2.

To protect your API key, you should not commit the ".env" file to source control. If you are using git, add ".env" to your ".gitignore" file, located in the "content-generator-app" folder.

This configures your app to use the OpenAI APIs through your platform account. We are now ready to implement the backend code.

6.6.4 Generating Content with the OpenAI APIs

To generate text, we will call the Chat API to use GPT-4o mini with the given prompt and return the generated response. Create the file "src/pages/api/generate-text.js" and enter the code in Listing 6-2.

Listing 6-2. Code for generate-text.js

```
import OpenAI from "openai";
// Initialise the OpenAI library to communicate with the
   OpenAI APIs
const openai = new OpenAI();
export default async function handler(req, res) {
   try {
      // Get the text prompt from the form
      const { prompt } = req.body;
      // Set up the system prompt and the prompt from
         the form
      const messages = [
         { role: "system", content: "Respond in a friendly
         tone."},
         { role: "user", content: prompt }
      ];
      // Generate the response to the prompt with GPT-4o mini
      const completion = await openai.chat.completions.create({
         messages: messages,
         model: "gpt-4o-mini",
         // The following parameters are optional and shown
         // to illustrate how to alter them
         max_tokens: 500,
         temperature: 1,
         top_p: 1,
```

CHAPTER 6   OVERVIEW OF THE OPENAI APIS

```
        frequency_penalty: 0,
        presence_penalty: 0
    });
    // Retrieve the response text
    const result = completion.choices[0].message.content;
    // Send the response text to display in the UI
    res.status(200).json({ result });
  } catch (error) {
    // Return an error message if the request failed
    res.status(500).json({ error: 'Failed to generate' });
  }
}
```

Let's break down what this code is doing. First, we initialize the OpenAI API library which automatically retrieves your API key from the ".env" file. In the handler function, we retrieve the *prompt* that the user typed in the form and then construct the prompts we will send to the Chat API, consisting of a system prompt with the instruction "Respond in a friendly tone," followed by the prompt given by the user.

Next, we call the Chat API to generate a response to our prompts. In addition to the prompts, the chat parameters including temperature and maximum tokens, described in Section 6.5.1, can also be configured. Once the response is received, it is sent to the UI to be displayed. To ensure any errors are handled gracefully, the code is wrapped with a try-catch block that returns the message "Failed to generate" in the event of a failure.

Once you have written the code, go back to your web app in your web browser, enter a prompt, for example, "Give me a haiku about apricots," and click "Generate Text." You should see the response displayed below the form, similar to Figure 6-12.

CHAPTER 6   OVERVIEW OF THE OPENAI APIS

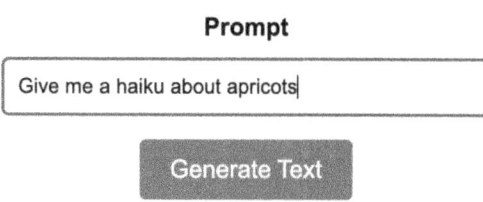

Figure 6-12. Example text content generated using the Chat API

To generate images, we will use the Image API to call DALL-E 3 with the given prompt and return the URL of the generated image to be displayed in the UI. Create the file "src/pages/api/generate-image.js" and enter the code in Listing 6-3.

Listing 6-3. Code for generate-image.js

```
import OpenAI from "openai";
// Initialise the OpenAI library to communicate with the
OpenAI APIs
const openai = new OpenAI();
export default async function handler(req, res) {
    try {
        // Get the image prompt from the form
        const { prompt } = req.body;
         // Generate the image
         const image = await openai.images.generate({
            model: "dall-e-3",
```

CHAPTER 6   OVERVIEW OF THE OPENAI APIS

```
            prompt: prompt,
            // The following parameters are optional and shown
            // to illustrate how to alter them
            quality: "standard",
            response_format: "url",
            size: "1024x1024"
        });
        // Retrieve the generated image URL
        const result = image.data[0].url;
        // Send the result to display in the UI
        res.status(200).json({ result });
    } catch (error) {
        // Return an error message if the request failed
        res.status(500).json({ error: 'Failed to generate' });
    }
}
```

Let's break down what this code is doing. We initialize the OpenAI library and extract the prompt provided in the UI in the same way as with text generation. We then call the Image API to generate an image from the prompt using DALL-E 3. Additional parameters including the size and quality of the image are also specified to illustrate how they can be adjusted. The generated image URL is then retrieved and sent to the UI to be displayed. The image URL is available for 1 hour after the image is generated.

Once you have written this code, return to your web app in your web browser, enter a prompt, for example, "A basket of apricots and pomegranates," and click "Generate Image." You should see the generated image displayed below the form, similar to Figure 6-13.

114

CHAPTER 6   OVERVIEW OF THE OPENAI APIS

Figure 6-13. Example image generated using the Image API

Experiment with different prompts by generating both text and images and adjusting the parameters for the Chat and Image APIs to see how they affect the outputs.

6.7 Summary

In this chapter, we introduced the OpenAI APIs, which allow us to integrate generative AI functionality into web applications. We gave an overview of the various APIs, focusing on the Chat API for generating text using GPT models, and the Image API for generating images using DALL-E. After covering the pricing and usage restrictions for each API, we set up an account on the OpenAI API platform, created a project, added credits, and created an API key to allow our web applications to use the APIs.

We then explored the Chat APIs through the OpenAI API Playground, where we experimented with different GPT models and adjusted parameters like temperature to compare outputs. Following this, we built a web app with Next.js to generate both text and images from a given prompt, utilizing the OpenAI Node.js library to communicate with the APIs.

In the next chapter, we'll review and compare alternative generative AI models from rival AI companies that compete with OpenAI.

CHAPTER 7

Alternative Models to OpenAI

7.1 Introduction

Following OpenAI's demonstration of generative AI's potential with the release of ChatGPT, numerous major tech firms shifted focus, and new startups emerged to develop rival alternatives. Though OpenAI initially held a significant technical lead, competitors have since closed the gap, with some even surpassing the performance of ChatGPT and DALL-E in certain areas. In this chapter, we will examine and compare the alternative options that have arisen for both text and image generation models.

7.2 Alternative Text Generation Models

Over a year after its release, ChatGPT held the top spot as the most capable and versatile large language model. However, since 2023, new competitors have emerged with models that rival, and occasionally surpass, the latest GPT models from OpenAI. In this section, we review the most noteworthy alternatives.

7.2.1 Google Gemini

In response to OpenAI's release of ChatGPT, Google launched its own competitor, Gemini,[1] in December 2023. Gemini comes in four versions: Nano, Flash, Pro, and Ultra. Nano is optimized for lightweight hardware such as mobile devices, Flash prioritizes speed, Pro focuses on output quality, and Ultra is designed for peak performance. As of August 2024, the Flash and Pro 1.5 models are considered the best for general use, offering multimodal capabilities and APIs for integration with apps. A unique feature of Gemini models is their long context length. Flash supports up to 1 million tokens, while Pro and Ultra can handle up to 2 million tokens – nearly 17 times the 120k context length of GPT-4o. This longer capacity allows the model to process and generate responses based on significantly larger datasets, which can be particularly useful for customization via Retrieval Augmented Generation (see Chapter 10).

Gemini does not perform as well as GPT-4o or other competitors in terms of benchmarks, but it isn't far behind.[2] Its key advantage lies in its integration with Google's broader product ecosystem, including Google Docs, Gmail, and other services. Additionally, Google is developing a tool called AI Studio, aimed at helping developers with prompt engineering, fine-tuning, and API integration (Figure 7-1).

---

[1] https://gemini.google.com/
[2] https://openai.com/index/hello-gpt-4o/

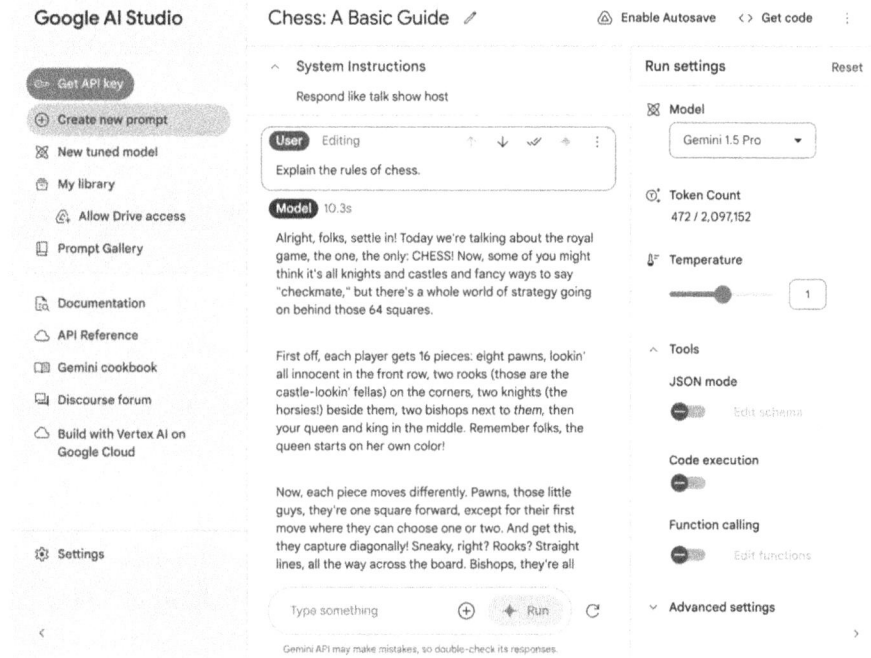

Figure 7-1. *Google AI studio for testing and building prompts with Gemini*

The Gemini APIs are priced competitively against GPT-4o models. Flash 1.5 costs half the price of GPT-4o mini up to 128k tokens (the maximum token limit of GPT-4o), Flash 1.5 is half the cost of GPT-4o mini for up to 128k tokens (the maximum token limit of GPT-4o), while Pro 1.5 is $2–5 cheaper than GPT-4o for the same token limit.[3] However, OpenAI's GPT-4o snapshot from 8 August 2024 is priced slightly lower than Pro 1.5, likely in response to Gemini's competitive pricing.[4]

---

[3] https://ai.google.dev/pricing
[4] https://openai.com/api/pricing/

Google is also entering the open source market with a family of models called Gemma,[5] which are based on its Gemini models. The latest release, Gemma 2, currently lags behind the performance of Meta's Llama models (see Section 7.2.3), but this is expected to improve as Google integrates advancements from its more recent Gemini developments.

Overall, Gemini is a strong contender worth considering, with performance close to rival models, competitive pricing, and a growing developer ecosystem. Its integration with Google's tools and the ongoing development of resources like AI Studio make it one of the best options for seamless integration.

7.2.2 Anthropic Claude

Anthropic, founded in 2021 by seven former OpenAI employees, develops an LLM called Claude, available in three editions: Haiku, Sonnet, and Opus. Haiku is optimized for lightweight tasks, Sonnet focuses on quality and performance, and Opus delivers the highest level of performance. The latest release, Claude Sonnet 3.5, outperforms GPT-4o in several benchmarks.[6] As of August 2024, Sonnet 3.5 is arguably the most capable general-purpose LLM, though this status may be short-lived as new models are released several times per year.

One of the standout features of Claude Sonnet is its *artifacts* side window which automatically renders outputs. For instance, if the output is a web page, the artifacts window runs the code, allowing you to interact with it live (see Figure 7-2). Additionally, artifacts update and refresh automatically as you prompt for edits, enabling you to see and verify changes in real time, making Claude Sonnet a versatile tool for prototyping and verification.

---

[5] https://ai.google.dev/gemma
[6] https://www.anthropic.com/news/claude-3-5-sonnet

CHAPTER 7   ALTERNATIVE MODELS TO OPENAI

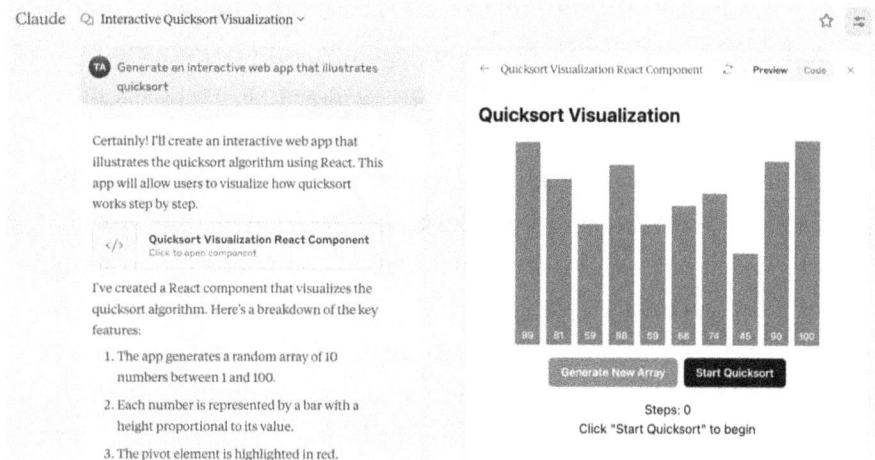

Figure 7-2. *Previewing a web app to illustrate quicksort with artifacts using Claude Sonnet 3.5*

All of Anthropic's LLMs, including Claude, are multimodal and come with API support. The API pricing for Claude 3.5 Sonnet is slightly more competitive than GPT-4o, offering a $2 discount per million input tokens, while the price for output tokens remains identical to GPT-4o.

Overall, Claude is a strong competitor to GPT-4o, currently outperforming it in certain benchmarks. The artifacts feature is a distinctive and practical tool, but it's relatively straightforward and likely to be adopted by rival platforms in the near future.

7.2.3 Meta LLama

In February 2023, Meta released the first version of their own large language model called LLama. However, unlike most other AI developers, Meta released its models open source, allowing anyone to run them on their own hardware. As of August 2024, the latest version, LLama 3.1, is available in three variants: 8B, 70B, and 405B. The 8B model is designed for

CHAPTER 7   ALTERNATIVE MODELS TO OPENAI

lightweight, simple tasks, the 70B variant is for more complex scenarios, and the 405B model delivers the highest quality outputs. Performance benchmarks for the 405B model are impressive, with its results coming close to GPT-4o and Claude Sonnet 3.5 across several metrics.[7]

The Llama models offer multimodal capabilities and are accessible via APIs through several cloud platforms, including AWS and Google Cloud. However, pricing is slightly higher than competing models, with the 405B version costing $0.30 more per million input tokens and $1 more per million output tokens compared to GPT-4o. The primary advantage of Llama is its open source distribution, making it an attractive choice for use cases where running models locally is preferred, such as for data protection or regulatory compliance. When Llama 3.1 was released, Mark Zuckerberg committed to keeping future Llama models open source, providing assurance to companies relying on the technology that it will remain supported for the long term.

Overall, Llama lags behind its rivals in performance, and its API access is slightly more expensive. However, its key advantage is its open source distribution, enabling companies to run the model on their own infrastructure. This makes it significantly easier to ensure compliance with data protection laws, a crucial benefit for many organizations.

7.2.4 Mistral

Mistral AI, a French startup founded in 2023 by former DeepMind and Meta engineers, is developing a series of LLMs also called Mistral, available in two editions: Nemo and Large 2. The Nemo model is designed for lightweight use cases, while Large 2 is aimed at more complex tasks. Mistral has also released two specialized models: Codestral for code generation and Embed for generating embeddings (see Chapter 10 for more on embeddings). The Nemo model is open source under the

---

[7] https://llama.meta.com/

Apache 2.0 license, allowing for commercial use, but the Large 2 model is not open source and requires direct negotiation with Mistral for commercial licensing.

The Large 2 model lags behind competitors like GPT-4o and Llama 3.1 in overall performance, but it excels in code generation and multilingual tasks.[8] Mistral's models are accessible through an API called "La Platforme," and the pricing is considerably more affordable than rival platforms, with Large 2 costing $2–6 less per million tokens compared to GPT-4o.

Overall, Mistral is still catching up in terms of model performance, which currently lags behind its rivals. However, as one of the newest generative AI companies, it shows promising potential. With further iterations, it is likely that their models will improve and become more competitive in the near future.

7.3 Alternative Image Generation Models

While DALL-E 3 is a versatile image generation model capable of producing a wide range of images, several competitive alternatives have emerged. In this section, we will review the two most well-known options: Stable Diffusion and Midjourney.

7.3.1 Stable Diffusion

Stable Diffusion, developed by Stability AI, is an open source image generation model available in three versions: Stable Diffusion 3 (SD3) with Medium and Large variants, Stable Diffusion XL (SDXL), and Stable Diffusion Ultra. While Stable Diffusion models perform well, they generally lack the same level of detail and quality as DALL-E 3 and Midjourney.

---

[8] https://mistral.ai/news/mistral-large-2407/

However, it is the best open source option, making it a good choice for those looking to run the model on their own infrastructure. In addition to generating images from scratch, Stable Diffusion offers a comprehensive range of features, including inpainting, removing backgrounds, and erasing objects.

The Stable Diffusion models can be accessed via a chatbot interface called Stable Assistant (see Figure 7-3), which offers a free three-day trial before requiring a paid subscription. The cheapest is the Standard subscription at $9 per month, allowing users to generate between 110 and 300 images depending on the quality. Stability AI also provides API access,[9] with pricing ranging from $0.035 per image for SD Medium to $0.08 per image for Ultra. This is comparable to DALL-E 3, which charges $0.04 for standard images and $0.12 for the highest quality (refer to Chapter 4, Section 4.2, for detailed DALL-E pricing). The API supports all the image editing, upscaling, and control features, offering more functionality than the DALL-E 3 API, which does not currently support image editing via API.

---

[9] https://platform.stability.ai/pricing

CHAPTER 7 ALTERNATIVE MODELS TO OPENAI

Figure 7-3. Generating images with Stability Assistant

Overall, Stable Diffusion is a competitive image generation model, with its key advantages over DALL-E 3 being its open source distribution, allowing users to generate images on their own infrastructure, and an API offering comprehensive image editing features. However, it is not able to produce the highest quality images that can be achieved on rival platforms like Midjourney.

7.3.2 Midjourney

Midjourney[10] is an independent research lab that develops an image generation AI of the same name. New versions are released frequently, with the latest being version 6.1 as of August 2024. Midjourney can be accessed through a web chat interface (see Figure 7-4) or via the messaging platform Discord. It offers public channels where users can generate images for free, but for private image generation, a paid subscription is required. Subscriptions start at $10 per month, allowing users to create approximately 200 images.

---

[10] https://www.midjourney.com/

CHAPTER 7   ALTERNATIVE MODELS TO OPENAI

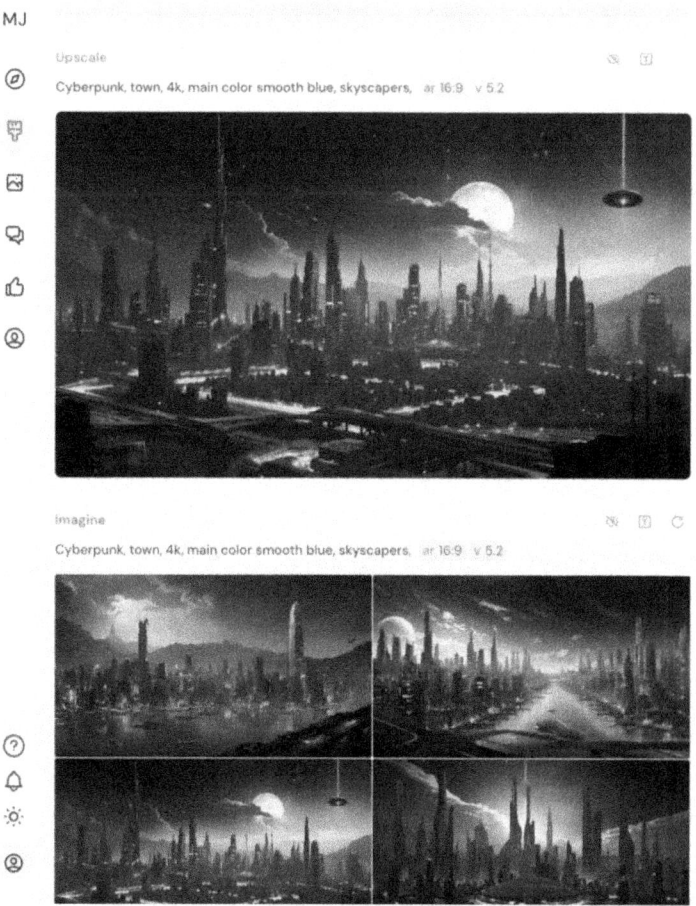

Figure 7-4. *Generating images with Midjourney through the web interface*

The main selling point of Midjourney is the quality of the images that it generates, which arguably beat all rival image generation models. Midjourney also provides a comprehensive set of image editing features including upscaling, zoom, and variations, making it comparable to Stable Diffusion in terms of functionality. Unfortunately, Midjourney does not provide an official API to generate images programmatically, limiting the ability to integrate it into applications.

CHAPTER 7 ALTERNATIVE MODELS TO OPENAI

Overall, Midjourney stands out as the highest quality image generation AI currently available. However, the absence of an official API limits the possibilities for integrating it into applications.

7.4 Summary

In this chapter, we reviewed alternative text and image generation AIs to OpenAI's ChatGPT and DALL-E. Since the release of ChatGPT, numerous companies have developed their own LLMs. While all of these models are built on the same underlying architecture – the transformer (see Chapter 1) – and generally offer similar features at comparable prices, a key distinction lies in their terms of use. GPT-4o, Gemini, and Claude are proprietary models, whereas Llama, Gemma, and Mistral Nemo are open source, providing more flexibility for those looking to run models on their own infrastructure.

The choice of which LLM to pick should be based on your long-term strategy for generative AI. If you are a Google user, Gemini is a compelling choice as it is being integrated into Google's suite of tools. For applications that require strict compliance with data privacy regulations, opting for an open source model like Llama, which can be run on your own infrastructure, may be the best approach, as it allows for full control and security of your data. Making a decision based on current benchmarks is not advisable, as AI companies are continuously improving and innovating and the title of best performing LLM changes too frequently. Similarly, choosing based on price is not likely to work long term, as intense competition is driving prices to similar levels across all platforms.

For image generation models, the choice primarily depends on the features you need. If image quality is the top priority and API access isn't necessary, Midjourney is the best option, offering the highest quality images along with a robust set of editing tools. If API access is required but only for image generation without the need for advanced editing,

CHAPTER 7 ALTERNATIVE MODELS TO OPENAI

DALL-E 3 provides good quality images at a competitive price. However, if data privacy is a concern, Stable Diffusion is the optimal choice, as it is open source and can be deployed on your own infrastructure, ensuring full control over your data.

In the remaining chapters of this book, we will focus on practical applications of generative AI by building web applications with Next.js and ChatGPT, incorporating features powered by the OpenAI APIs.

PART II

Building Generative AI–Powered Web Apps

CHAPTER 8

Building a Story/Poetry Generator

8.1 Introduction

In this chapter, we turn our attention to the practical application of the concepts we've explored so far. Our aim is to use generative AI to create a web application that generates unique stories, poems, and songs, together with AI-generated illustrations. By the end of this chapter, you will have a fully functional Next.js web app, a deeper understanding of OpenAI's API capabilities, and an improved ability to leverage AI in your web development projects.

We will build this project throughout the chapter step by step. However, if you wish to view or refer to the completed projects, the source code for this book is available on GitHub via the book's product page, located at www.apress.com/9798868808845.

8.2 Setting Up the Project

Before setting up the project, ensure you have Node.js LTS installed. Refer to Chapter 5, Section 5.2, for instructions on how to do this.

CHAPTER 8   BUILDING A STORY/POETRY GENERATOR

To create the project, open a terminal and run the following command:

> *npx create-next-app@latest story-generator-app*

You will be prompted with the following questions on how to configure the project. To match the example in this book, answer the questions the same way. If you configure the project differently, you may need to modify the code examples to be compatible:

1. Would you like to use Typescript: **No**/Yes
2. Would you like to use ESLint: **No**/Yes
3. Would you like to use Tailwind CSS: **No**/Yes
4. Would you like to use "src/" directory: No/**Yes**
5. Would you like to use App Router: **No**/Yes
6. Would you like to customize the default import alias: **No**/Yes

After completing these commands, the project will be created in a folder called *story-generator-app*.

Next, in your terminal, change to the project folder by running:

> *cd story-generator-app*

and then install two libraries: the OpenAI API library for communicating with the OpenAI APIs and sqlite3 which we will use as a database for saving the stories:

> *npm install openai sqlite3*

CHAPTER 8 BUILDING A STORY/POETRY GENERATOR

Additionally install the Prisma library which we will use to save our stories to the SQLite database:

> *npm install prisma --save-dev*

Finally, delete the template code that we don't need so that it doesn't interfere with our project:

1. First, **delete** the following files:
    - src/styles/globals.css
    - src/styles/Home.module.css
    - src/pages/api/hello.js
    - public/next.svg
    - public/vercel.svg

2. Then, open "src/pages/index.js" and delete all the content so it is a blank file.

3. Finally, open "src/pages/_app.js" and **delete** the first line *import "@/styles/globals.css";*.

8.2.1 Configuring an OpenAI API Key

To integrate chat functionality into our project, we need to configure our app to use the OpenAI APIs. In Chapter 6, we set up an OpenAI account, created a project, and then generated an API key. If you don't have an API key, follow the steps in Chapter 6 to obtain one and copy it. Then, in your web app, create a new file called ".env" in the root of your project (Figure 8-1) and write the following:

OPENAI_API_KEY=sk-xxx

CHAPTER 8 BUILDING A STORY/POETRY GENERATOR

Replacing "sk-xxx" with your generated OpenAI API key.

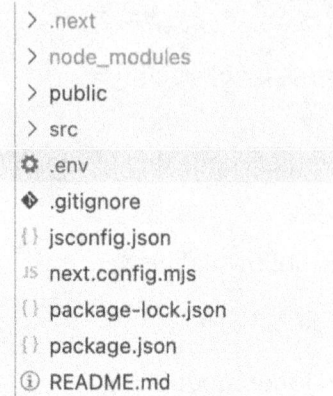

Figure 8-1. *Creating the .env file for the OpenAI API key*

To protect your API key, you should not commit the ".env" file to source control. If you are using git, add ".env" to your ".gitignore" file located in the story-generator-app folder.

This completes the setup of our project.

8.3 Creating the UI

To generate a story with ChatGPT, we first need to collect some inputs that will determine what the story is about. We will collect three pieces of information:

1. The name of the main character
2. A description of the plot
3. A description of the ending

After the user has entered these details in a form, we will have a "Generate" button below that when clicked sends these inputs to ChatGPT which generates the story and then returns it. We will then display the story beneath the form.

CHAPTER 8   BUILDING A STORY/POETRY GENERATOR

To generate the page, open a new chat in ChatGPT and ensure that ChatGPT-4o or 4o-mini is selected. Then paste and run the prompt in Listing 8-1.

Listing 8-1. Prompt for creating the story generator UI

```
I'm writing a web page in React using NextJS. The page has
an HTML form to collect three text inputs: "main character",
"plot", and "ending". The form has a submit button with text
"Generate".
The submit button will be disabled when the form is submitted
and re-enabled when submission has finished. When the form is
submitted an onSubmit method is called which calls a REST API
using the "fetch" function with endpoint url "api/generate-
story". Each of the three inputs are sent as a POST request in
the body as JSON.
The response from this API will be the story. The API returns
the story as JSON in a property called "story". Display this
story as text underneath the form. Include some CSS styles
inline to make it look modern. Output all of the code as a
single file.
```

Let's step through this prompt one paragraph at a time and understand what it is doing:

> *"I'm writing a web page in React using NextJS. The page has an HTML form to collect three text inputs: "main character", "plot", and "ending". The form has a submit button with text "Generate"."*

The first sentence describes to ChatGPT the task we are trying to perform, generating a web page in React using Next.js. This is important as it provides ChatGPT with context of the programming languages and

CHAPTER 8   BUILDING A STORY/POETRY GENERATOR

frameworks we are using. If we simply said "I want to generate a web page," ChatGPT might generate code for a different framework. The second sentence describes the HTML form and the inputs we want to have. Notice we specify the types of the inputs are *text*, not numbers, images, or something else. We also put the names of the types in quotes as this makes it unambiguous to ChatGPT what they should be called. Finally, we specify that there should be a submit button.

> *"The submit button will be disabled when the form is submitted and re-enabled when submission has finished. When the form is submitted an onSubmit method is called which calls a REST API using the "fetch" function with endpoint url "api/generate-story". Each of the three inputs are sent as a POST request in the body as JSON."*

When the submit button is clicked, we don't want the user to be able to click it again until the story has finished generating, so we specify that it should be disabled when the form is submitted and re-enabled when the story has finished generating. To generate the story with our inputs, we will run a function (called an API endpoint) that we will write later and that will call ChatGPT to generate the story, and the name of this API endpoint is "generate-story". To help ChatGPT generate the correct code, we describe briefly the technical details for how to call our API function: using a built in JavaScript function called "fetch" and passing the story inputs in JSON (JavaScript Object Notation) format.

> *"The response from this API will be the story. The API returns the story as JSON in a property called "story". Display this story as text underneath the form. Include some CSS styles inline to make it look modern. Output all of the code as a single file."*

CHAPTER 8   BUILDING A STORY/POETRY GENERATOR

To help ChatGPT generate valid code, we again briefly describe the technical details of how the generated story will be returned: our API returns some JSON containing a property called "story" whose value is the generated story. We then ask ChatGPT to provide some CSS styles to make the appearance modern. Feel free to experiment with different style descriptions such as "retro," "minimalist," and "colorful." Finally, we specify that all the code, the HTML, JavaScript, and CSS, be combined into a single file. Keeping all the code in one file makes it easy to copy/paste the output from ChatGPT and test it, but later, you may prefer to put the styles into a separate CSS file so they can be reused among other pages in your app.

In ChatGPT's response, you should receive a single block of code that contains all the logic for the page like in Figure 8-2. If you receive more than one block of code, respond with the following prompt: "Give me all the code as a single file." Then, copy and paste all the code into a new file "*src/pages/story-generator.js*".

```
Here's a complete React component in a single file that implements your requirements using Next.js.
```

```jsx
import { useState } from 'react';

export default function StoryGenerator() {
  const [mainCharacter, setMainCharacter] = useState('');
  const [plot, setPlot] = useState('');
  const [ending, setEnding] = useState('');
  const [story, setStory] = useState('');
  const [isSubmitting, setIsSubmitting] = useState(false);

  const handleSubmit = async (event) => {
    event.preventDefault();
    setIsSubmitting(true);

    const requestBody = {
      mainCharacter,
      plot,
      ending,
```

Figure 8-2. Generated code for the story generator UI

Chapter 8 Building a Story/Poetry Generator

Let's take a look at what the UI looks like. In a terminal, start your website if it isn't already running:

> *npm run dev*

In a web browser, navigate to *http://locahost:3000*, and you should see a page that should be something similar to Figure 8-3.

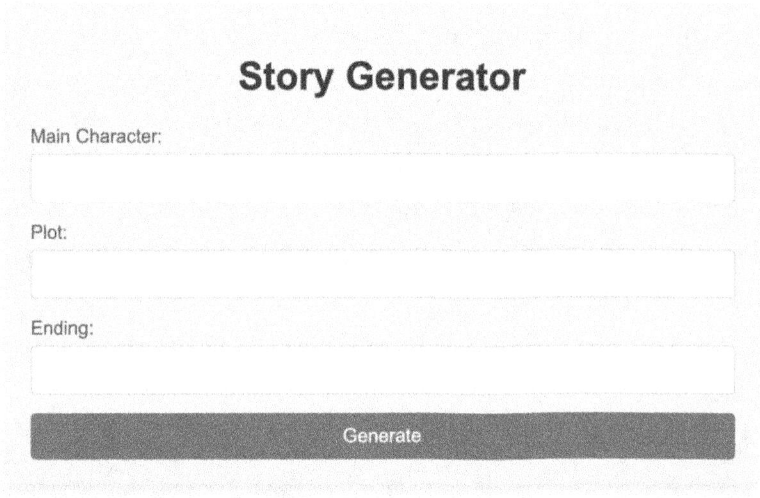

Figure 8-3. *Story generator UI*

If your form doesn't look well formatted, it's possible ChatGPT didn't generate any CSS. To fix this, go back to the chat in ChatGPT and respond with a prompt: "Add some inline CSS to make the appearance modern. Output all the code as a single file." Sometimes, ChatGPT doesn't respect all of the requests in our prompt, and we have to remind it of the things it forgot in follow-up prompts.

This UI is a great start, but currently, when we click "Generate," nothing happens because there is no code to generate the story. In the next section, we will generate the backend logic so our story gets generated and displayed.

CHAPTER 8   BUILDING A STORY/POETRY GENERATOR

8.4 Creating the Backend

We have a UI to collect the inputs for our story, but currently nothing happens when we click generate because we haven't yet implemented the "generate-story" function. In this section, we will use ChatGPT to help write the backend code to do this.

8.4.1 Generating the Story

To get ChatGPT to generate a story, we need to give it a prompt that describes what it should be. Since creating good prompts is hard, let's get ChatGPT to write it for us. Open the same chat that we used to generate the frontend code, and run the following additional prompt:

> *Generate a prompt for ChatGPT to generate a story using the parameterized inputs: main character, plot, and ending. It should instruct ChatGPT to create a story between 300 and 400 words and must use all of the three inputs. Include instructions to make the story unique and detailed. The prompt should be a single paragraph of text. Output the prompt as a javascript template string and no other information.*

The response should be something similar to the code in Listing 8-2.

Listing 8-2. Generated code for the story prompt

```
const prompt = `Create a unique and detailed story between 300 and 400 words that includes the following elements: a main character described as ${mainCharacter}, a plot involving ${plot}, and an ending where ${ending}. Ensure that the story is engaging, with vivid descriptions and a clear narrative structure that ties together all three components in a creative way.`;
```

Now that we have a prompt, we can generate the backend code that will utilize it. In order to explain how the OpenAI API works, we're going to write this code step by step, rather than get GPT to generate it, but in your subsequent projects, you can avoid the manual code writing by crafting your own prompt to generate the code.

First, create a new file "*src/pages/api/generate-story.js*". In this file, we're going to write a function that receives the three inputs, the main character, plot, and ending, generates the story with GPT, and then returns it. Let's first get the three inputs, shown in Listing 8-3.

Listing 8-3. Getting the story inputs from the UI

```
import OpenAI from "openai";
const openai = new OpenAI();
export default async function handler(req, res) {
    // Get the inputs for the story
    const { mainCharacter, plot, ending } = req.body;
    // Replace with your prompt
    const prompt = <your prompt>;
}
```

First, we import the OpenAI library and then create an instance of it that we will later use to call ChatGPT. Then, we define our function which receives a "req" (request) parameter containing all the inputs and a "res" (response) parameter we can use to return the generated story. We then extract the main character, plot, and ending from the request and construct our prompt, where you should paste the prompt you generated from ChatGPT earlier.

Now, let's generate the story with GPT-4o using the code shown in Listing 8-4.

CHAPTER 8   BUILDING A STORY/POETRY GENERATOR

Listing 8-4. Generating the story with the Chat API

```
export default async function handler(req, res) {
    // ... previous code ...
    try {
        // Generate the story with GPT-4o
        const completion = await openai.chat.completions.create({
            messages: [
                { role: "system", content: "You are a creative
                story writer." },
                { role: "user", content: prompt }
            ],
            model: "gpt-4o",
        });
        const story = completion.choices[0].message.content;
        res.status(200).json({ story });
    } catch (error) {
        res.status(500).json({ error: 'Failed to generate
        story' });
    }
}
```

We've wrapped the code that generates the story in a try-catch block which will handle any errors that occur by returning the message "Failed to generate story" using the "res" parameter with HTTP status code 500 which indicates an error.

Inside the try block, we call the "openai.chat.completions.create" function and provide it a list of two messages. The messages are prompts in the same manner that we write to ChatGPT, only here in addition to the message content we can also specify a "role." Roles allow us to have more complex interactions with GPTs, but for now, we will only use "system" and "user." The *system* role can be used to configure the behavior of the GPT by providing an initial prompt that describes how the GPT should respond to future messages in this chat (see Chapter 3, Section 3.4.2). In our example, we've configured the GPT with the prompt "You are a creative story writer." The *user* role represents messages sent by the user, and in our example, we're providing the prompt to generate the story. Once the story is generated, we extract it from the list of generated completions and return it as JSON using the "res" parameter with HTTP status code 200 which indicates success.

Once you have written this code, try running your website, navigate to `http://localhost:3000/story-generator` in your web browser, enter the three inputs for the story into the form, and click "Generate." After a few seconds, you should see your generated story appear below the form such as the example in Figure 8-4.

CHAPTER 8   BUILDING A STORY/POETRY GENERATOR

Story Generator

Main Character:

Ani

Plot:

Falls into a rabbit hole and enters a magical kingdom

Ending:

Becomes queen and lives happily ever after

Generate

Ani often found herself lost in the pages of her favorite adventure books. Life in her small village was quaint but unremarkable, and she yearned for something extraordinary. Little did she know, the extraordinary was about to find her.

One warm afternoon, Ani explored the woods behind her house, hoping to discover a hidden gem or secret trail. As the sun filtered through the trees, casting dappled shadows on the forest floor, she stumbled upon an old oak tree with a peculiar, glittering rabbit by its base. Fascinated, she crouched down to get a better look. Suddenly, the ground beneath her gave way, and she found herself plummeting into darkness.

When Ani landed, she was bewildered but unharmed. She found herself in a bewildering land where colors were more vibrant, and the very air seemed to shimmer with magic. Before her stood a bustling kingdom, inhabited by enchanting creatures and talking animals. Awestricken, she ventured into the heart of this magical kingdom.

Ani quickly made friends, from the eloquent fox named Reynard to the

Figure 8-4. Example of a generated story

Experiment with different inputs, and see what kind of stories are being generated. In general, the stories are not high quality, but with some extra customization to the prompts, we can make them more interesting.

CHAPTER 8　BUILDING A STORY/POETRY GENERATOR

8.5 Generating Different Types of Literature

With only three inputs: main character, plot, and ending, there is a limit to how much we can customize our stories. In this section, we are going to add two additional inputs to our story generator: *genre*, for example, "crime," "adventure," "romantic," "thriller," etc., and *literature*, for example, "story," "poetry."

8.5.1 Generating Different Genres

Adding an additional input to the story generator UI can be achieved easily by getting ChatGPT to update our existing code. To do this, open "src/pages/story-generator.js", select all the text in the file, and copy it to the clipboard. Next, open a *new chat* in ChatGPT, and enter and run the prompt in Listing 8-5, pasting the code below the prompt text.

Listing 8-5. Prompt to add a "genre" input for the story generator

```
Add a select to the form in this Next.JS page to choose the
genre of the story. Populate the select with 10 story genres.
Send the selected genre in the API request to 'generate-story'.
Give me the entire code with all the modifications as one file.
<paste code here>
```

After running this prompt, you should receive the modified code for the page. If ChatGPT doesn't give you all the code, try running the prompt again or responding with another prompt "Give me the entire code as one file." Copy and paste the code into "story-generator.js", replacing the code that is already in this file. You should see that we are passing a new input "genre" to "generate-story" as in Figure 8-5.

CHAPTER 8   BUILDING A STORY/POETRY GENERATOR

Here is the modified code that adds a select dropdown to choose the style of the story, populates it with 10 story genres, and sends the selected genre in the API request to `generate-story`:

```javascript
import { useState } from 'react';

export default function StoryGenerator() {
  const [mainCharacter, setMainCharacter] = useState('');
  const [plot, setPlot] = useState('');
  const [ending, setEnding] = useState('');
  const [genre, setGenre] = useState('Fantasy');
  const [story, setStory] = useState('');
  const [isSubmitting, setIsSubmitting] = useState(false);

  const handleSubmit = async (event) => {
    event.preventDefault();
    setIsSubmitting(true);

    const requestBody = {
      mainCharacter,
      plot,
      ending,
      genre,
    };
```

Figure 8-5. *Updated UI code with the new "genre" input*

Next, we need to modify "generate-story.js" to use the new "genre" input. Modify the code in "generate-story.js" as shown in Listing 8-6.

Listing 8-6. Code modifications to add the "genre" input to generate-story.js

```
// ... previous code ...
export default async function handler(req, res) {
    // Get the inputs for the story
    const { mainCharacter, plot, ending, genre } = req.body;
    const prompt = `... rest of prompt ... The genre of the
    story is ${genre}.`;
//   ... rest of the code ...
```

CHAPTER 8   BUILDING A STORY/POETRY GENERATOR

Here, we collect the genre input and add an additional sentence to the prompt specifying the genre.

Now, run your website and try generating stories and selecting different genres. An example is shown in Figure 8-6.

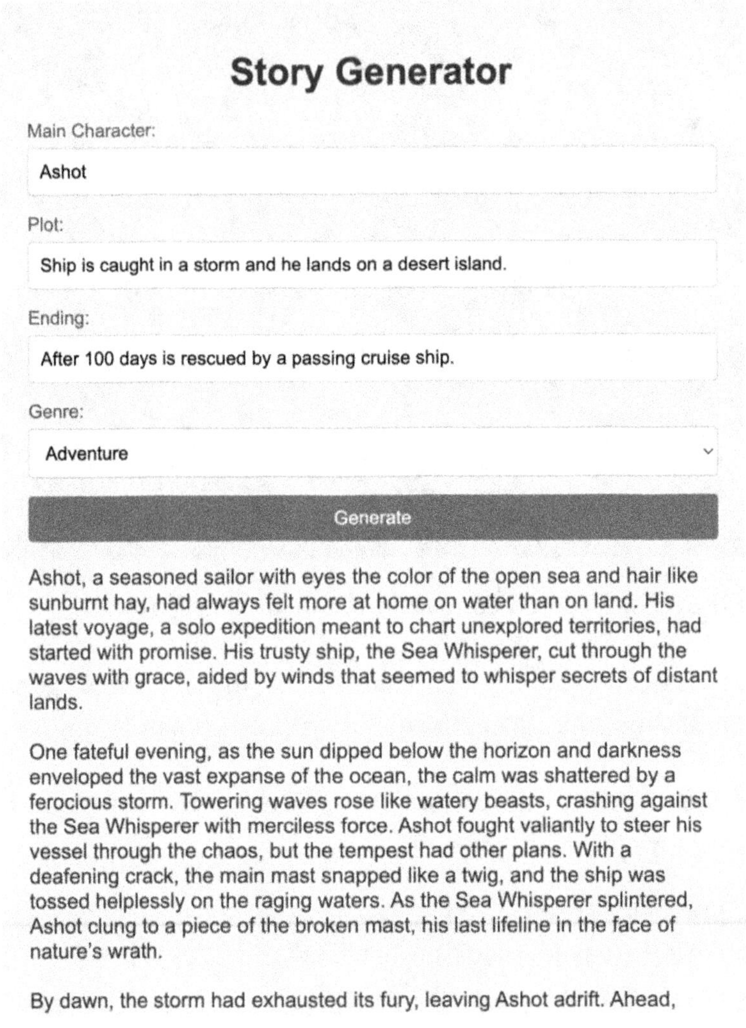

Story Generator

Main Character:
Ashot

Plot:
Ship is caught in a storm and he lands on a desert island.

Ending:
After 100 days is rescued by a passing cruise ship.

Genre:
Adventure

[Generate]

Ashot, a seasoned sailor with eyes the color of the open sea and hair like sunburnt hay, had always felt more at home on water than on land. His latest voyage, a solo expedition meant to chart unexplored territories, had started with promise. His trusty ship, the Sea Whisperer, cut through the waves with grace, aided by winds that seemed to whisper secrets of distant lands.

One fateful evening, as the sun dipped below the horizon and darkness enveloped the vast expanse of the ocean, the calm was shattered by a ferocious storm. Towering waves rose like watery beasts, crashing against the Sea Whisperer with merciless force. Ashot fought valiantly to steer his vessel through the chaos, but the tempest had other plans. With a deafening crack, the main mast snapped like a twig, and the ship was tossed helplessly on the raging waters. As the Sea Whisperer splintered, Ashot clung to a piece of the broken mast, his last lifeline in the face of nature's wrath.

By dawn, the storm had exhausted its fury, leaving Ashot adrift. Ahead,

Figure 8-6. *A generated adventure story*

8.5.2 Generating Poetry

To generate other types of literature such as poetry, we can follow the same process we used to add the *genre* input to add a *literature* input. Open "src/pages/story-generator.js", select all the text in the file, and copy it to the clipboard. Next, open a *new chat* in ChatGPT, and enter the prompt in Listing 8-7, pasting your code below the prompt text.

Listing 8-7. Prompt to add a "literature" input to the story generator UI

```
Add a select to the form in this Next.JS page to choose the
'literature' type. Populate the select with the two options
'story' and 'rhyming poetry'. Send the selected 'literature' in
the API request to 'generate-story'. Give me the entire code
with all the modifications as one file.
<paste your code here>
```

After running this prompt, you should receive the modified code for the page containing a new input with the option to choose between "story" and "rhyming poetry." If ChatGPT doesn't give you all the code, try running the prompt again or responding with another prompt "Give me the entire code as one file." Copy and paste the code into "story-generator.js", replacing the code that is already in this file.

Next, we need to modify "src/pages/api/generate-story.js" to use the new *literature* input. Modify the code in "generate-story.js" to extract the "literature" input from the request, and then in the prompt, replace any occurrences of the word "story" with the token "${literature}" as shown in the example code in Listing 8-8.

CHAPTER 8 BUILDING A STORY/POETRY GENERATOR

Listing 8-8. Code modifications to add the "literature" input to generate-story.js

```
// ... previous code ...
export default async function handler(req, res) {
    // Get the inputs for the story
    const { mainCharacter, plot, ending, genre, literature } = req.body;

    // Replace with your prompt:
    const prompt = `Create a unique and detailed ${literature} between 300 and 400 words that includes the following elements: a main character described as ${mainCharacter}, a plot involving ${plot}, and an ending where ${ending}. The genre of the ${literature} is ${genre}. Ensure that the ${literature} is engaging, with vivid descriptions and a clear narrative structure that ties together all three components in a creative way.`;
// ... rest of the code ...
```

Once you have made these changes, try generating some rhyming poetry such as in the example in Figure 8-7.

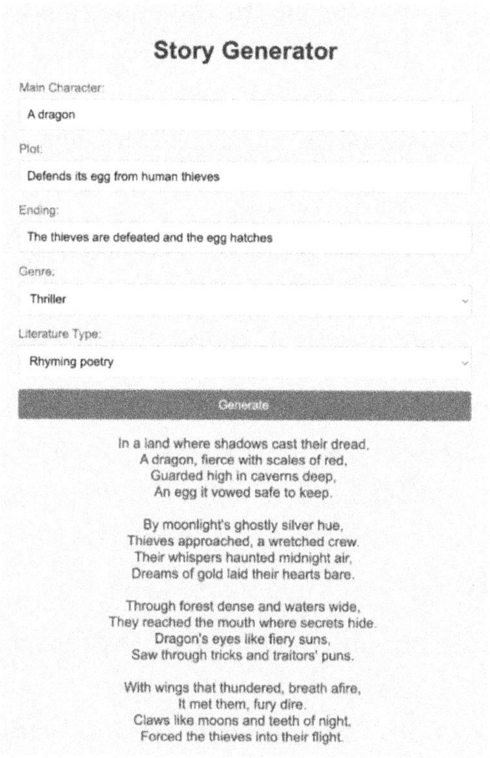

CHAPTER 8   BUILDING A STORY/POETRY GENERATOR

Story Generator

Main Character:
A dragon

Plot:
Defends its egg from human thieves

Ending:
The thieves are defeated and the egg hatches

Genre:
Thriller

Literature Type:
Rhyming poetry

[Generate]

In a land where shadows cast their dread,
A dragon, fierce with scales of red,
Guarded high in caverns deep,
An egg it vowed safe to keep.

By moonlight's ghostly silver hue,
Thieves approached, a wretched crew.
Their whispers haunted midnight air,
Dreams of gold laid their hearts bare.

Through forest dense and waters wide,
They reached the mouth where secrets hide.
Dragon's eyes like fiery suns,
Saw through tricks and traitors' puns.

With wings that thundered, breath afire,
It met them, fury dire.
Claws like moons and teeth of night,
Forced the thieves into their flight.

Figure 8-7. Example of generated poetry

You can follow this process to add even more inputs, for example, additional characters and plot lines, the language, etc.

We can now generate stories and poetry and have the ability to customize them with additional inputs. In the next section, we will generate illustrations with DALL-E.

8.6 Generating Illustrations

To generate illustrations for our stories, we will use the Image API (see Chapter 5 for an introduction to DALL-E and Chapter 6 for an introduction to the Image API). We will do this in two steps, first modifying the UI code

CHAPTER 8 BUILDING A STORY/POETRY GENERATOR

with the help of ChatGPT to display the illustration alongside the story and second modifying "generate-story.js" to additionally generate and return the illustration.

To modify the UI code, open "src/pages/story-generator.js", select all the code and copy it to the clipboard. Then, open a *new chat* in ChatGPT and enter the prompt in Listing 8-9, pasting your code below the prompt text.

Listing 8-9. Prompt to modify the UI to display the illustration

```
The 'generate-story' endpoint in this Next.JS page additionally
returns  illustrationb64 with the image in base64 format.
Modify the page to display the image inline with the story.
Give me the entire code with all the modifications as one file.
<paste your code here>
```

After running this prompt, you should receive the modified code for the page. If ChatGPT doesn't give you all the code, try running the prompt again or responding with another prompt "Give me the entire code as one file." Copy and paste the code into "story-generator.js", replacing the code that is already in this file.

To generate the illustration, we will follow this strategy:

1. Generate the story text with the Chat API.

2. Then, send another prompt to generate a description of the illustration for the story.

3. Give this description of the illustration to the Image API to generate it.

4. Return the story and illustration as base64. Base64 format allows us to easily transfer and store the image (see Section 8.8).

CHAPTER 8 BUILDING A STORY/POETRY GENERATOR

Open "src/pages/api/generate-story.js" and make the modifications shown in Listing 8-10.

Listing 8-10. Code to generate illustrations with DALL-E in generate-story.js

```
// ... previous code ...
export default async function handler(req, res) {
    // ... code as before ...
    try {
        const messages = [
            { role: "system", content: "You are a creative
            story writer." },
            { role: "user", content: prompt }
        ];
        // Generate the story with GPT-4o
        const completion = await openai.chat.completions.
        create({
            messages: messages,
            model: "gpt-4o",
        });
        const story = completion.choices[0].message.content;
        // Add the generated story to the list of messages
        messages.push(completion.choices[0].message);
        // Now add a message to generate a prompt for
        generating the illustration
        messages.push({ role: "user", content: "Now give me a
        short prompt for an illustration for this story I can
        provide to DALL-E 3. Output the prompt and no other
        information." });
        // Generate the prompt that describes the illustration
        we want to generate with DALL-E
```

CHAPTER 8   BUILDING A STORY/POETRY GENERATOR

```
        const dallePromptCompletion = await openai.chat.
        completions.create({
            messages: messages,
            model: "gpt-4o",
        });
        const dallePrompt = dallePromptCompletion.choices[0].
        message.content;
        // Generate the illustration
        const illustration = await openai.images.generate({
            model: "dall-e-3",
            prompt: dallePrompt,
            response_format: "b64_json"
        });
        const illustrationb64 = illustration.data[0].b64_json;
        res.status(200).json({ story, illustrationb64 });
    } catch (error) {
        res.status(500).json({ error: 'Failed to generate
        story' });
    }
}
```

After generating the story, we add the generated story text to the list of messages followed by another prompt: "Now give me a short prompt for an illustration for this story I can provide to DALL-E 3. Output the prompt and no other information." Adding the generated story text to the list of messages allows the GPT to generate an illustration prompt inspired by the content of the story, rather than just from the original story prompt. We then call "openai.images.generate" to generate the illustration with DALL-E 3 using our generated image prompt. Finally, we return both the story and illustration in base64 format to be displayed in our UI.

CHAPTER 8   BUILDING A STORY/POETRY GENERATOR

After you have made these modifications, try generating some new stories and check if the illustrations are suitable. An example is shown in Figure 8-8. Note that the illustration URLs returned by the Image API only work for one hour after they were generated.

Figure 8-8. *A generated story with an illustration*

Our story generator is now able to generate literature based on our inputs along with an illustration. Following the methodology in this section, additional images could be generated, for example, illustrating the beginning, middle, and ending of the story.

8.7 Adding a Library Page

We have built a story generator that creates stories and poetry, but every time we refresh or navigate away from the page, we lose the stories that we generated. In this section, we'll save our stories to a SQLite database and create a library page to view them.

8.7.1 Saving the Stories

To save the stories, we will use a lightweight database called SQLite,[1] which allows us to store our stories in a structured format. We'll use a library called Prisma[2] to simplify setting up the database, adding new stories, and reading the saved ones for display on the library page.

First, we'll set up Prisma and our database. To do this, open a terminal in the story-generator folder and run the following command:

> *npx prisma init --datasource-provider sqlite*

This will create a new folder in our project called *prisma* containing a file *schema.prisma*. In this file, we specify the name of the database and the schema of the tables. Open this file, and modify its contents to match Listing 8-11.

---

[1] https://www.sqlite.org/
[2] https://www.prisma.io/

CHAPTER 8   BUILDING A STORY/POETRY GENERATOR

Listing 8-11. Contents of prisma.schema

```
// This is your Prisma schema file,
// learn more about it in the docs: https://pris.ly/d/
prisma-schema

generator client {
  provider = "prisma-client-js"
}

datasource db {
  provider = "sqlite"
  url      = env("DATABASE_URL")
}

model Story {
  id              String   @id @default(cuid())
  text            String
  illustrationb64 String
}
```

In this file, we've defined a model called Story which contains three columns: an ID, the story text, and the base64-encoded illustration.

Next, we will configure the name of the database. Open your ".env" file in the "story-generator-app" folder, and modify the environment variable "DATABASE_URL" as follows:

```
DATABASE_URL="file:./stories.db"
```

With the database configuration written, we can now create the database. In a terminal within the "story-generator-app" folder, run the following command:

```
> npx prisma db push
```

In the console output, you should see the "*stories.db*" database is created and a message "Generated Prisma Client" indicating the command succeeded. This completes the creation of the database.

In order to use the database in our code, we need to create an instance of the Prisma Client library. Due to the way Next.js works internally, it's best practice to create a single instance of the client, as recommended in the Next.js documentation.[3] To do this, create the file "src/lib/prisma.js", also creating the "lib" folder if it doesn't exist. In this file, write the code provided in Listing 8-12.

Listing 8-12. Code to create the prisma instance in "lib/prisma.js"

```
import { PrismaClient } from '@prisma/client'
const prismaClientSingleton = () => {
  return new PrismaClient()
}
const prisma = globalThis.prismaGlobal ?? prismaClientSingleton()
export default prisma
if (process.env.NODE_ENV !== 'production') globalThis.prismaGlobal = prisma
```

When our project is running development mode, such as when we run "*npm run dev*," we create and return a single instance of the Prisma Client.

Now, we are ready to save the stories into our database. Open "src/pages/api/generate-story.js" and make the modifications shown in Listing 8-13.

---

[3] https://www.prisma.io/docs/orm/more/help-and-troubleshooting/help-articles/nextjs-prisma-client-dynamic

CHAPTER 8   BUILDING A STORY/POETRY GENERATOR

Listing 8-13. Saving the stories in generate-story.js

```
import OpenAI from "openai";
import prisma from '@/lib/prisma';
const openai = new OpenAI();
// ... rest of the code ...
      const illustrationb64 = illustration.data[0].b64_json;
      // Save the story to the database
      await prisma.story.create({
          data: {
              text: story,
              illustrationb64: illustrationb64
          }
      });
      res.status(200).json({ story, illustrationb64 });
// ... rest of the code ...
```

First, we import the Prisma Client from the file prisma.js we created earlier. Then, after generating the illustration for the story, we call the client to save the story text and illustration in the "Story" table in our database.

With our stories now being saved, we can proceed to build a library page to display them.

8.7.2 Building the Library UI

Our library page will feature a simple interface that allows users to view the story text and the illustration, with "Previous" and "Next" buttons to browse through the stories stored in the database. Like with the other UIs in this project, we will generate it with ChatGPT. To begin, open ChatGPT, create a new chat, and paste and run the prompt in Listing 8-14.

CHAPTER 8   BUILDING A STORY/POETRY GENERATOR

Listing 8-14. Prompt for generating the UI for the library page

```
I'm writing a web page in React using NextJS. The page will be
used to display stories which consist of the story text and the
image in base64 format.
The stories can be retrieved using Primsa. The schema for the
data is as follows:
model Story {
  id      String   @id @default(cuid())
  text    String
  illustrationb64 String
}
You can import the prisma client by using:
import prisma from '@/lib/prisma';
On the web page add previous and next buttons to navigate
through the stories. Add some css using nice fonts to make the
stories look authentic using the styled-jsx tag.
Output all the code as a single file.
```

Let's break down what this prompt is doing. First, it describes the behavior of the library page, displaying both stories and images. Then, it explains how to retrieve the stories using the Prisma library, utilizing the schema and Prisma client code we developed. Following this, it specifies that there should be Previous and Next buttons and the website should be styled to make the stories look authentic. The styling should be implemented using the styled-jsx in accordance with Next.js best practices. Finally, it states that the code should be output as a single file to make it easy to edit and put into our project.

After running this prompt, you should have a single block of code. Copy it and paste it in a new file "src/pages/library.js". Once complete, run your website and generate two or three stories. Then, navigate to the library page at http://localhost:3000/library to view them. Figure 8-9 shows an example of the library page with some generated poetry.

CHAPTER 8   BUILDING A STORY/POETRY GENERATOR

In the garden so fair, under leaves that weave,
Lived a bright caterpillar with dreams up his sleeve.
He met a small beetle, shiny and sleek,
Together they'd journey to the faraway creek.

They crawled through the meadows, the paths seldom seen,
Through blossoms of purple and grasses so green.
On their way, spiders and ants joined their quest,
New friends in their travels, all eager and zest.

At last by the creek, in the soft gleam of dusk,
They unearthed hidden shells, in glittery husk.
With treasures in tow, and their friendship in bloom,
They returned to their world, dispelling all gloom.

Figure 8-9. Example poetry displayed in the library page

This completes the implementation of the library page.

We've created a page for generating stories and a library for viewing them. To complete the app, we will create a simple home page to navigate easily between these two pages.

8.8 Creating a Home Page

We've developed two pages for our story generator: one to generate stories and another for viewing them. However, the only way to navigate to them is by manually entering their URLs in the address bar, which isn't particularly user-friendly. To improve this, we'll create a simple home page with two circular tiles to navigate between the two pages. To create it, open ChatGPT and begin a new chat. Then, write the prompt in Listing 8-15 and run it.

Listing 8-15. Prompt for generating the home page

```
I'm writing a web page in React.js with Next.js using the pages
router. I'm creating a homepage that contains two circular
tiles centered both vertically and horizontally on the middle
of the page and spaced a bit apart. The border of the tiles is
medium thick, one is green and the other is blue. When hovering
over these tiles there is a shadow effect that makes the tiles
lift off the page. The text inside the first tile is "Generate
Story" and the text inside the other text tile is "View
Library". When clicking on the first tile the page navigates
to the url '/story-generator' and when clicking on the second
tile the page navigates to '/library'. Use the next router to
navigate between pages.
Add some css using the styled-jsx tag to make the page
look modern with a light theme. Output all the code as a
single file.
```

The prompt describes the layout and content of the home page in a step-by-step manner. When the prompt completes, you should receive a single block of generated code. Copy it and paste it into "src/pages/index.js". To view the home page, run the web app and navigate to

CHAPTER 8 BUILDING A STORY/POETRY GENERATOR

http://localhost:3000/. An example is displayed in Figure 8-10. If the page does not appear correctly or throws an error, then regenerate the code by regenerating the prompt in ChatGPT.

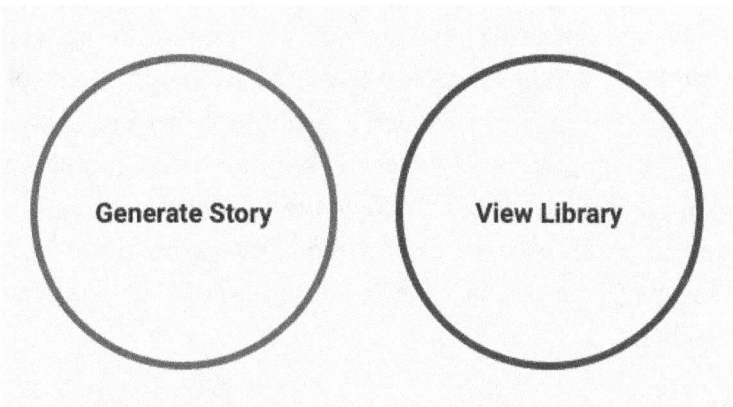

Figure 8-10. *Example navigation tiles on the home page*

This completes the implementation of our story generator app. To improve the app further, consider implementing the following enhancements:

1. Generate titles for the stories and display them in the library page.

2. Improve the user interface by making the styles between pages consistent and adding additional navigation between them.

3. Create multiple illustrations for the stories.

4. Generate longer form stories consisting of multiple chapters.

CHAPTER 8   BUILDING A STORY/POETRY GENERATOR

8.9 Summary

In this chapter, we built a story generator web app with Next.js that uses the Chat API to write stories and poetry based on the user's inputs and generates illustrations using the Image API. We learned how to modify our app to add extra inputs and customize it to generate a variety of types of literature. Furthermore, we created a database to save our stories and developed a library page to view them. Finally, we built a simple home page to make it easy to navigate between the two pages.

In the next chapter, we will explore more ways to build web applications with ChatGPT and the OpenAI APIs by building a language learning web app.

CHAPTER 9

Building a Language Learning App

9.1 Introduction

Learning a new language can be challenging and requires regular practice in speaking, reading, and writing. ChatGPT, having been trained on an extensive dataset comprising text from the Internet and various books, has proficiency in several languages other than English. As of August 2024, GPT-4o supports over 50 languages ranging from Spanish and French to Japanese and Arabic.[1] An important aspect of language acquisition is the memorization of vocabulary. In this chapter, we will build a language learning web app using Next.js. The app will use ChatGPT to generate quizzes for learning vocabulary, grading the responses, and providing constructive feedback.

We will build this project throughout the chapter step by step. However, if you wish to view or refer to the completed projects, the source code for this book is available on GitHub via the book's product page, located at www.apress.com/9798868808845.

---

[1] https://help.openai.com/en/articles/8357869-how-to-change-your-language-setting-in-chatgpt#h_513834920e

CHAPTER 9 BUILDING A LANGUAGE LEARNING APP

9.2 Setting Up the Project

Before setting up the project ensure you have Node.js LTS installed. Refer to Chapter 5, Section 5.2, for instructions on how to do this.

To create the project, open a terminal and run the following command:

> *npx create-next-app@latest language-learning-app*

You will be prompted with the following questions on how to configure the project. To match the example in this book, answer the questions the same way. If you configure the project differently, you may need to modify the code examples to be compatible:

1. Would you like to use Typescript: **No**/Yes
2. Would you like to use ESLint: **No**/Yes
3. Would you like to use Tailwind CSS: **No**/Yes
4. Would you like to use "src/" directory: No/**Yes**
5. Would you like to use App Router: **No**/Yes
6. Would you like to customize the default import alias: **No**/Yes

After completing these commands, the project will be created in a folder called *language-learning-app*.

Next, in your terminal, change to the project folder by running:

> *cd language-learning-app*

and then install two libraries that we will use: OpenAI to use the APIs and zod for validating JSON objects:

> *npm install openai*

Finally, delete the template code that we don't need so that it doesn't interfere with our project:

1. First, **delete** the following files:
   - src/styles/globals.css
   - src/styles/Home.module.css
   - src/pages/api/hello.js
   - public/next.svg
   - public/vercel.svg

2. Then, open "src/pages/index.js" and delete all the content so it is a blank file.

3. Finally, open "src/pages/_app.js" and **delete** the first line *import "@/styles/globals.css";*.

9.2.1 Configuring an OpenAI API Key

To integrate ChatGPT functionality into our web app, we will use the OpenAI APIs. In Chapter 6, we set up an OpenAI account, created a project, and then generated an API key. If you don't have an API key, follow the steps in Chapter 6 to obtain one and copy it. Then in your web app, create a new file called ".env" in the root of your project (Figure 9-1) and write the following:

OPENAI_API_KEY=sk-xxx

Replacing "sk-xxx" with your generated OpenAI API key.

CHAPTER 9   BUILDING A LANGUAGE LEARNING APP

Figure 9-1. *Creating the .env file for the OpenAI API key*

To protect your API key, you should not commit the ".env" file to source control. If you are using git, add ".env" to your ".gitignore" file located in the *language-learning-app* folder.

This completes the setup of our project.

9.3 Creating a Vocabulary Translating Quiz

A useful method for practicing and learning vocabulary is through a multiple-choice quiz, where you are given a word in a foreign language and must choose the correct translation. If you choose incorrectly, a mnemonic is provided to aid in remembering the word. In this section, we'll create this interactive quiz using the Chat API to generate the questions, answers, and feedback.

9.3.1 Building the Backend

We'll start by building the backend functionality of our application, which will be the following:

CHAPTER 9 BUILDING A LANGUAGE LEARNING APP

1. **Language Selection:** The user specifies the *language* they would like to practice and the *vocabulary category* – the types of words they would like to have a quiz on, for example, clothing, furniture, transport, etc.

2. **Generate Quiz:** The Chat API will be used to generate a series of ten multiple-choice questions, each with four choices and one correct answer. Each question will also have a helpful mnemonic to display if the user answers the question incorrectly. The Chat API will return the response as JSON so the UI can process the questions and display them.

3. **Return Quiz:** The quiz is returned to the UI so the user can do the quiz.

Now, let's build the backend logic in stages. Create the file "src/pages/api/generate-translating-quiz.js" and enter the code in Listing 9-1.

Listing 9-1. Skeleton code for generate-translating-quiz.js

```
import OpenAI from "openai";
import { z } from "zod";
import { zodResponseFormat } from "openai/helpers/zod";
// Initialise the OpenAI library to communicate with the OpenAI APIs
const openai = new OpenAI();
export default async function handler(req, res) {
    try {
```

CHAPTER 9 BUILDING A LANGUAGE LEARNING APP

```
    } catch (error) {
        // Return an error message if the request failed
        res.status(500).json({ error: "Failed to generate
        quiz" });
    }
}
```

First, we import a few functions and libraries and instantiate the OpenAI client to access the Chat API. Next, we define our function which receives a "req" (request) parameter containing all the inputs and a "res" (response) parameter we can use to return the generated quiz. To handle any potential errors during the process, we've included a try-catch block. If an error occurs, the catch block will ensure that a message – "Failed to generate quiz" – is returned with an HTTP status code of 500, indicating an internal server error.

Now that we have the skeleton of our backend code, let's implement the logic that generates the quiz. In order to make it easy for our code to process the quiz questions, choices, and mnemonics, we will employ the Chat API to generate our quiz in a structured format. Both GPT-4o and GPT-4o mini are capable of returning their output in JSON format following a schema provided along with the prompt. To generate this schema, we will use a library called "zod" that simplifies the process of describing our data format. Enter the code in Listing 9-2 at the start of the "try" block.

Listing 9-2. Creating the QuizTemplate JSON schema in zod

```
// ... previous code ...
try {
        // The template for the quiz
        const QuizTemplate = z.object({
            quizQuestions: z.array(
                z.object({
                    question: z.string(),
```

CHAPTER 9   BUILDING A LANGUAGE LEARNING APP

```
            choices: z.array(z.object({
                id: z.number(),
                text: z.string()
            })),
            answerId: z.number(),
            mnemonic: z.string()
          })
        )
    });
// ... rest of the code ...
```

In the code in Listing 9-2, we define our schema *QuizTemplate* to have a *quizQuestions* property containing an array of question objects each with a *question, choices, answerId,* and *mnemonic.* Each choice has an *ID* and *text.* We can now use this schema with the Chat API to generate the quiz. Enter the code in Listing 9-3 immediately below the *QuizTemplate* definition.

Listing 9-3. Generating the quiz with the Chat API

```
// ... previous code ...
// Set up the system prompt and generate the quiz.
const messages = [
    { role: "system", content: "You are a professional
    language coach who is a master at creating multiple choice
    vocabulary quizzes to practise learning words. Each quiz
    you create is exactly 10 questions long, with 4 choices
    and exactly 1 correct answer. Each question is a single
    word in the foreign language and vocabulary category
    specified, and the options are possible translations of the
    word in english. All of the choices for a given word must
    be different. Each question also has a mnemonic that the
    student can use to memorise the correct translation if they
    answer the question wrong."},
```

```
    { role: "user", content: `Give me a quiz to learn Clothing
    in Spanish.` }
];
// Generate the response to the prompt with GPT-4o mini
const completion = await openai.chat.completions.create({
    messages: messages,
    model: "gpt-4o-mini",
    response_format: {
        type: "json_schema",
        json_schema: zodResponseFormat(QuizTemplate,
        "quiz").json_schema
    }
});
// Retrieve and parse the quiz
const quiz = JSON.parse(completion.choices[0].message.content);
// Send the quiz data back to the UI.
res.status(200).json(quiz);
// ... rest of the code ...
```

First, we create a list of messages that we will send to the Chat API. The *system prompt* describes the task of generating the quiz, and to help get high-quality results, we define the persona to be a professional language coach who is a master at creating quizzes. Next, we outline the format of the quiz, specifying that we want four choices that are possible translations of the word. To avoid repeating the same question multiple times, we state that the choices should be different. The second message with the *user* role then requests the GPT to generate a quiz to learn clothing vocabulary in Spanish. For now, we have hard-coded the vocabulary and language so we can verify the output of our function. Later, we'll update these values based on the incoming request.

Next, we call the Chat API to generate the quiz, passing along our list of messages along with an additional parameter *response_format*, where we specify our quiz template JSON schema. The *response_format* parameter

CHAPTER 9   BUILDING A LANGUAGE LEARNING APP

is a newer feature, and as of August 2024, it's only supported by the models: "*gpt-4o-mini*," "*gpt-4o-mini-2024-07-18*," and "*gpt-4o-2024-08-06*." In this example, we are using "*gpt-4o-mini*," but if you wish to use the more powerful GPT-4o model, you'll need to change the model value to "*gpt-4o-2024-08-06*." Check the Chat API reference page for any updates on supported models.[2] Once the Chat API processes the request, the quiz is returned as JSON with HTTP status code 200, indicating success.

Let's test out this function to see what the output looks like. Open a terminal and in the language-learning-app folder, run the following command to start the app:

```
> npm run dev
```

The terminal output will display the URL where the website is running, typically defaulting to http://localhost:3000. Open a web browser, and in the address bar, enter the following URL and navigate to the page: http://localhost:3000/api/generate-translating-quiz. It will take several seconds to load as the quiz is generated. Once the page finishes loading, you should see the JSON object for the quiz containing questions such as the one shown in Listing 9-4.

Listing 9-4. Example generated quiz question for learning Spanish words for clothing

```
"quizQuestions": [
    {
        "question": "Camisa",
        "choices": [
            {
```

---

[2] https://platform.openai.com/docs/guides/structured-outputs/introduction

```
                "id": 1,
                "text": "Shirt"
            },
            {
                "id": 2,
                "text": "Pants"
            },
            {
                "id": 3,
                "text": "Skirt"
            },
            {
                "id": 4,
                "text": "Hat"
            }
        ],
        "answerId": 1,
        "mnemonic": "Think of 'camisole' which is a type
        of shirt."
    },
    ...
]
```

This shows us that the output is being generated correctly. In order to generate quizzes for other languages and vocabulary categories, return to the code for "generate-translating-quiz.js" and modify it as shown in Listing 9-5.

CHAPTER 9 BUILDING A LANGUAGE LEARNING APP

Listing 9-5. Modifying generate-translate-quiz.js to use the provided language and category

```
// ... previous code ...
try {
        // Get the options from the form
        const { language, category } = req.body;
        // The template for the quiz
        const QuizTemplate = // .. template as before
        // Set up the system prompt and generate the quiz.
        const messages = [
            { role: "system", content: // content as before },
            { role: "user", content: `Give me a quiz to learn
            ${category} in ${language}.` }
        ];
// ... rest of code ...
```

The code in Listing 9-5 fetches the language and category from the UI and inserts them into the prompt used to generate the quiz.

This completes the implementation of the backend. In the next section, we will create the UI to interact with the quiz.

9.3.2 Implementing the UI

To implement the UI, we will get ChatGPT to write a simple one for us. The high-level design of the UI will be

1. **Language Selection:** The user will be prompted to pick from nine languages.
2. **Category Selection:** Next, the user will select from nine vocabulary categories.

3. **Quiz Generation:** Generate the quiz while showing a progress spinner.

4. **Quiz Presentation:** Present each quiz question one at a time, specifying the word that should be translated along with four buttons, one for each answer choice.

5. **Answer Feedback:** If the user answers correctly, the choice button will be highlighted green. Otherwise, it will be highlighted red and the correct answer button highlighted green, with the mnemonic displayed underneath.

6. **Quiz Summary:** After answering all ten quiz questions, a summary will be displayed showing how many questions were answered correctly. The incorrect words will be displayed along with their mnemonics.

To generate this page, open ChatGPT and create a new chat. This prompt works best with ChatGPT 4o, so if you have a ChatGPT Plus subscription, be sure to enable it. However, if you are using ChatGPT 4o mini, you may not get good results running the entire prompt at once. In this case, you may have more success entering the prompt in stages so that the page is built incrementally. Enter and run the prompt in Listing 9-6. This is a complex prompt that describes in detail the UI behavior we outlined. We encourage you to read through it to understand what it is doing.

CHAPTER 9 BUILDING A LANGUAGE LEARNING APP

Listing 9-6. Prompt for ChatGPT to generate the UI for the translating quiz

```
I'm writing a web page in React.js with Next.js using the pages
router. I'm going to describe how to write the code for this
in steps:
1. The page first displays a series of 9 tiles (displayed in a
3x3 grid) for selecting one of the following nine languages:
'French', 'German', 'Spanish', 'Italian', 'Greek', 'Japanese',
'Korean', 'Mandarin', 'Arabic'.
2. When the language is selected the tiles disappear and the
user sees another 9 tiles to choose one of the following
vocabulary categories: 'Clothing', 'Furniture', 'Transport',
'Food', 'Animals', 'Colors', 'Numbers', 'Body parts', 'School'.
3. When the user selects the category the tiles disappear and
a REST POST API call is made using the fetch function to the
endpoint '/api/generate-translating-quiz' to generate a quiz,
passing the 'language' from the react state variable, and
'category' just selected in the body as JSON.
4. While the REST API call is executing, display a CSS progress
spinner in the middle of the page (remember to include
keyframes to make it spin).
5. The API returns a JSON object that contains the quiz
questions, four choices, the answer, and a mnemonic. The schema
of this JSON object is the following expressed as the following
zod object:
z.object({
    quizQuestions: z.array(
        z.object({
            question: z.string(),
            choices: z.array(z.object({
                id: z.number(),
```

CHAPTER 9   BUILDING A LANGUAGE LEARNING APP

```
            text: z.string()
        })),
        answerId: z.number(),
        mnemonic: z.string()
    })
  )
})
```

6. The UI then displays each quiz question with the label text "Translate this word {question}" followed by the question. There are four buttons, arranged in a 1x4 layout, underneath for the user to pick their choice.
7. If the user picks the correct answer, as specified in the 'answerId', then the button the user clicked changes color to green while the other buttons go grey. Additionally when the user answers correctly, a message is also displayed saying 'Well done!'. Make sure only the color of the button changes, not the rest of the style.
8. If the user picks the wrong answer, the color of the button the user clicked changes to red, and the button corresponding to the correct color is highlighted green. Additionally when the user answers incorrectly, the mnemonic is displayed to help the user remember the word.
9. When the user clicks one of the choices, the buttons for the choices are disabled and not clickable for that question. Instead a next button appears and the app waits for the user to click it to proceed to the next question.
10. There will be exactly 10 questions to answer.
11. At the end of the quiz a summary is displayed showing how many questions the user got correct, which words the user didn't get right, and the mnemonics for those words. Format the summary nicely. There is then a button for the user to go back to the language selection part and begin a new quiz.

CHAPTER 9   BUILDING A LANGUAGE LEARNING APP

```
12. Add CSS using the styled-jsx tag to make the interface
modern using a light color palette. All of the content should
be centered on the page.
Output all of the code as a single file.
```

In steps 1 and 2, we provide a list of specific languages and vocabulary categories and describe how the user picks them. Steps 3 and 4 explain how to generate the quiz using the "api/generate-translating-quiz" function. While the function is running a CSS spinner. We also included a remark "remember to include keyframes to make it spin" because when testing this prompt, ChatGPT regularly forgot to include this piece of CSS code to make the spinner animated. When constructing your own prompts like this, or modifying existing ones, you may have to "remind" ChatGPT of certain facts that it frequently doesn't take into account. It's not always clear why certain tasks are trickier than others, and the reasons are likely to do with what was most prevalent in the training data for ChatGPT.

Step 5 describes the format of the quiz returned by "generate-translating-quiz" where we provide the structure of the JSON object using the "zod" notation from our code. Steps 6–9 explain how the UI behaves when displaying the quiz, where the user is given four choices for each question. Steps 10 and 11 explain how to display a summary at the end of the quiz. Step 12 describes how to add CSS styles to the generated page to give it a "modern" style using a light color palette. The remark to use "the styled-jsx tag" to output the CSS is to force ChatGPT to use the recommended way of adding CSS in Next.js.

Once the code is generated, copy it and paste it into a new file "src/pages/translating-quiz.js". Then, start the web app, and in your browser, navigate to `http://localhost:3000/translating-quiz`. You should have a functioning interface to play the quiz, an example of which is in Figure 9-2. Your UI may look different as ChatGPT does not generate the same code each time.

If the app throws an error at any stage during the quiz or behaves incorrectly, return to ChatGPT, start a new chat, paste the original prompt, and regenerate the code. Be aware that there are some recurring issues that ChatGPT might not handle correctly when generating the page:

1. The spinner isn't generated or doesn't spin.
2. The quiz answers are already shown when viewing the questions.
3. The correct quiz answers are not shown when you answer incorrectly.
4. When reaching the end of the quiz, an error is thrown rather than going to the summary page.
5. The summary page does not show the questions that were incorrectly answered.

In all of these cases, either regenerate the page with ChatGPT until it produces a page that functions correctly or follow up with a prompt describing the behavior that doesn't work, pasting any error messages and asking ChatGPT to fix it. To make it easier to update the code, ask ChatGPT to give you the complete code with the changes made. You should get a functioning page within two or three attempts.

CHAPTER 9   BUILDING A LANGUAGE LEARNING APP

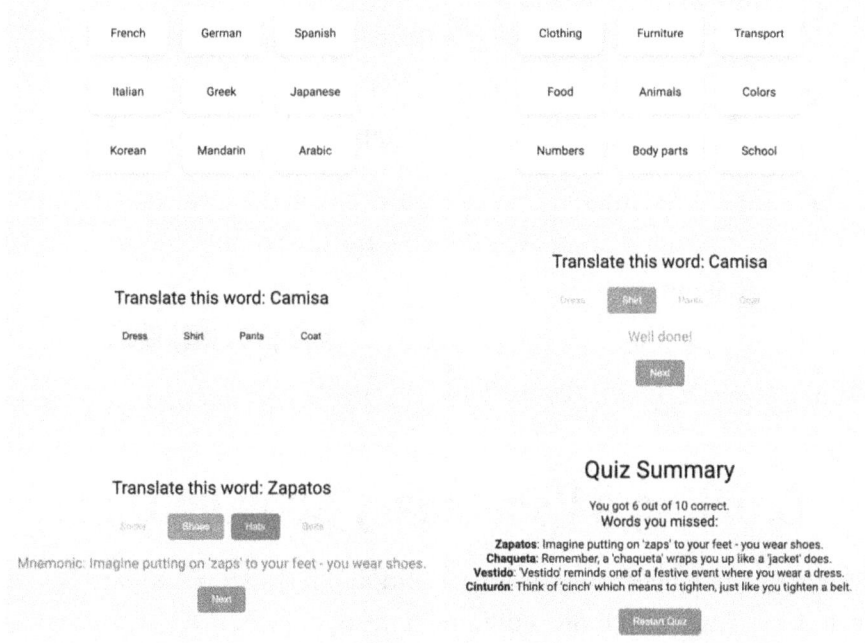

Figure 9-2. *Six screens showing playing a quiz in the vocabulary learning page*

Try playing a few quizzes, and see what parts of the application work well and which require improvement. Using the techniques from Chapter 5, try improving the appearance and adding new features to the app, for example, you can ask ChatGPT to:

- Adjust the CSS to a color scheme, fonts, and layout to your preferences.

- Add animations when you transition between questions.

- Allow the user to specify any language and vocabulary category of their choice.

- Have different levels of difficulty so that there are different word selections each time the quiz is run.

- Set up a pass/fail threshold, and keep track of which quizzes have been passed and failed.

- Keep a record of the words you've covered in previous quizzes, and don't include them the next time you run the same quiz.

In the next section, we will implement a different kind of vocabulary learning quiz that tests your knowledge of spellings.

9.4 Creating a Vocabulary Spelling Quiz

In the previous section, we created a multiple-choice quiz for learning vocabulary. Now, we'll build a different type of quiz focused on testing spelling knowledge. Our app will generate a list of words in the selected language and vocabulary category. Then, using DALL-E, we will generate an image that represents each word. In each quiz question, we will display the images and ask the user to write the corresponding word in the chosen language. We will then evaluate their spelling and show them mnemonics to help them remember if they spelled the word incorrectly.

9.4.1 Building the Backend

We'll begin by creating another backend function that will generate the quiz. The functionality will be the following:

1. **Language Selection:** The user specifies the *language* they would like to practice and the *vocabulary category* – the types of words they would like to have a quiz on, for example, clothing, furniture, transport, etc.

CHAPTER 9   BUILDING A LANGUAGE LEARNING APP

2. **Generate Quiz:** The Chat API will be used to generate four questions consisting of a word in the selected language, a description of the image in English that can be given to DALL-E, and a mnemonic to help remember the word if the user gets it wrong.

3. **Generate Images:** For each quiz question, an image representing the word will be generated using the image prompt created for DALL-E. The images will then be stored with the quiz questions.

4. **Return Quiz:** The quiz is returned to the UI so the user can play it.

Let's build this in steps. Create the file "src/pages/api/generate-spelling-quiz.js" and enter the code in Listing 9-7.

Listing 9-7. Skeleton code for generate-spelling-quiz.js

```
import OpenAI from "openai";
import { z } from "zod";
import { zodResponseFormat } from "openai/helpers/zod";
// Initialise the OpenAI library to communicate with the
OpenAI APIs
const openai = new OpenAI();
export default async function handler(req, res) {
    try {

    } catch (error) {
        // Return an error message if the request failed
        res.status(500).json({ error: "Failed to generate
        quiz" });
    }
}
```

CHAPTER 9   BUILDING A LANGUAGE LEARNING APP

This is the same template code we started with in Section 9.3.1. We import libraries for communicating with the OpenAI APIs and instantiate the OpenAI client. Our function receives the request and response parameters and contains a try-catch block for handling errors.

We can now implement the logic that generates the quiz questions which we will generate in the same manner as Section 9.3.1, providing a JSON schema to the Chat API to return results in the specified format. Enter the code in Listing 9-8 at the start of the "try" block.

Listing 9-8. Generating the spelling quiz questions

```
// ... previous code ...
// Get the options from the form
const { language, category } = req.body;
// The template for the quiz
const QuizTemplate = z.object({
    quizQuestions: z.array(
        z.object({
            question: z.string(),
            imagePrompt: z.string(),
            mnemonic: z.string()
        })
    )
});
// Set up the system prompt and generate the quiz.
const messages = [
    { role: "system", content: "You are a professional language
    coach who is a master at creating vocabulary quizzes to
    practise learning words. Each quiz you create is exactly
    4 questions long, and consists of a question which is
    a single word in the specified language and vocabulary
    category. Each question must be a different word. For each
```

CHAPTER 9   BUILDING A LANGUAGE LEARNING APP

```
    question you will also provide an imagePrompt written in
    english that is a single short simple phrase that can be
    given to DALL-E to generate an image that represents the
    question word. Each question also has a mnemonic that the
    student can use to memorise the word if they answer the
    question wrong."},
    { role: "user", content: `Give me a quiz to learn
${category} in ${language}.` }
];
// Generate the response to the prompt with GPT-4o mini
const completion = await openai.chat.completions.create({
    messages: messages,
    model: "gpt-4o-mini",
    response_format: {
        type: "json_schema",
        json_schema: zodResponseFormat(QuizTemplate, "quiz").
        json_schema
    }
});
// Retrieve and parse the quiz
const quiz = JSON.parse(completion.choices[0].message.content);
// ... rest of the code ...
```

In the code in Listing 9-8, we define a schema QuizTemplate containing an array of quiz questions, where each question has the question text, image prompt, and mnemonic. Then, we create the list of messages that we will send to the Chat API. The system prompt describes how we will generate the quiz. With this quiz, we will generate just four questions. Generating images with DALL-E is expensive, both in terms of computation time and financial cost. On the Tier 1 plan for the OpenAI APIs, DALL-E 2 is rate limited to five images per minute (see Chapter 6). To save costs and not hit the rate limit, four questions is a compromise. We

CHAPTER 9   BUILDING A LANGUAGE LEARNING APP

specify that the imagePrompt be written in English because DALL-E does not perform as well with other languages. We then call the Chat API with the list of messages using gpt-4o-mini, providing our JSON schema and parsing the result.

Now that we have generated our list of questions, we can generate the images for them. Enter the code in Listing 9-9 immediately below the code that generates the quiz questions.

Listing 9-9. Generating the images for the spelling quiz

```
// ... previous code ...
// For each question generate an image with DALL-E
const imagePromises = quiz.quizQuestions.map(q => openai.images.generate({
    model: "dall-e-2",
    prompt: q.imagePrompt,
    response_format: "b64_json",
    size: "256x256"
}));
// Wait for all the images to be generated
const imageResults = await Promise.all(imagePromises);
// Add the base64 image to each quiz question
imageResults.forEach((result, index) => {
    quiz.quizQuestions[index].imageb64 = result.data[0].b64_json;
});
// Send the quiz data back to the UI.
res.status(200).json(quiz);
// ... rest of the code ...
```

In the code in Listing 9-9, we loop over all the quiz questions and call the Image API to generate an image with DALL-E 2 using the image prompt generated. We are using DALL-E 2 with an image resolution of 256×256 as this is the fastest and cheapest image generation API. We could generate high-quality images with DALL-E 3, but these would take a lot longer to generate and be more expensive. We also set the *response_format* to "b64_json" which stands for "base64 json". Base64 is an encoding that encodes binary data into plaintext. This format is particularly useful if you need to store images in JSON or another text-based format. It means we can send the images to the UI in the same JSON as the rest of the quiz questions, making them more convenient to process. We generate all four images, one for each of the four questions, in parallel, and once generated, save them in the quiz questions in a property called imageb64. Finally, we return the quiz data with HTTP status code 200 indicating the quiz was generated successfully.

If you wish to test this function out like we did in Section 9.3.1 for the other quiz generator, hard-code the values for the *language* and *category*, for example, to "Spanish" and "clothing," and then in your browser, navigate to `http://localhost:3000/api/generate-spelling-quiz` to generate the output.

This completes the implementation of the backend. In the next section, we will create the UI to interact with the quiz.

9.4.2 Implementing the UI

To implement the UI, we will get ChatGPT to write a basic one for us. The high-level design will be

1. **Language Selection:** The user will be prompted to pick from nine languages.

2. **Category Selection:** Next, the user will select from nine vocabulary categories.

3. **Generate Quiz:** Generate the quiz while showing a progress spinner.

4. **Quiz Presentation:** Present each image one at a time, and provide a text box for the user to write the translation of the word to the selected language.

5. **Quiz Feedback and Summary:** After the user provides their answers to all four images, a summary will be displayed showing which images they correctly translated. The incorrect translations will be displayed along with their mnemonics to help the user remember them.

To generate this page, open ChatGPT and create a new chat. This prompt works best with ChatGPT-4o, so if you have a ChatGPT Plus subscription, be sure to enable it. If you are using ChatGPT 4o mini, you may not get good results running the whole prompt at once. Instead, you may have more success adding the prompt a few steps at a time so that the page is built incrementally. Enter and run the prompt in Listing 9-10.

Listing 9-10. Prompt for ChatGPT to generate the UI for the spelling quiz

```
I'm writing a web page in React.js with Next.js using the pages
router. I'm going to describe how to write the code for this
in steps:
1. The page first displays a series of 9 tiles (displayed in a
3x3 grid) for selecting one of the following nine languages:
'French', 'German', 'Spanish', 'Italian', 'Greek', 'Japanese',
'Korean', 'Mandarin', 'Arabic'.
2. When the language is selected the tiles disappear and the
user sees another 9 tiles to choose one of the following
vocabulary categories: 'Clothing', 'Furniture', 'Transport',
'Food', 'Animals', 'Colors', 'Numbers', 'Body parts', 'School'.
```

3. When the user selects the category all the tiles are hidden, and a REST POST API call is made using the fetch function to the endpoint '/api/generate-spelling-quiz' to generate a quiz, passing the 'language' which MUST come from the react state variable, and the 'category' just selected in the body as JSON.
4. While the REST API call is executing, display a CSS progress spinner in the middle of the page (remember to include keyframes to make it spin).
5. The API returns a JSON object that contains the quiz questions, the base64 image, and a mnemonic. The schema of this JSON object expressed as the following zod object:
```
z.object({
    quizQuestions: z.array(
        z.object({
            question: z.string(),
            imagePrompt: z.string(),
            imageb64: z.string(),
            mnemonic: z.string()
        })
    )
})
```
6. The UI then displays each base64 image WITHOUT revealing the question word along with the label text "Write the name of this object in {language}". There is a form with a textbox centered below the image where the user can type their answer, and a "Next" button below the textbox to submit their answer and go to the next question. When the user clicks "Next" to move to the next question, and clear the textbox and put the focus on it.
7. There are exactly 4 questions to answer.

CHAPTER 9   BUILDING A LANGUAGE LEARNING APP

8. After the four questions have been answered, for each question compare what the user typed with the "question" word. If they are equal, ignoring case, then the user got it right. If they are different the user got it wrong. Display a result summary showing all the images and the questions the student got right and those they got wrong. For the questions they got wrong the mnemonic will also be displayed. There is a button for the user to go back to the language selection part and begin a new quiz.
9. Add CSS using the styled-jsx tag to make the interface modern using a light color palette. All of the content should be centered on the page.
Output all of the code as a single file.

This is a complex prompt that describes the UI behavior, and we encourage you to read it to understand how it works and how to write complex prompts. Steps 1 and 2 are the same as from Section 9.3.2 and describe how the user selects the language and vocabulary category from a selection of nine choices. Steps 3 and 4 describe how to call the generate-spelling-quiz function we created for the backend, showing an animated spinner while the function is executing. Step 5 describes the format of the quiz returned. In the zod JSON object definition, we added the "imageb64" field for the base64 encoded image which gets added after the Chat API has generated the quiz questions.

Step 6 describes how to display each question to the user, one image at a time without revealing the question word to the user. The word "WITHOUT" is written in uppercase to signify to the GPT that it is an essential requirement. This is a useful technique more generally; even highlighting words with asterisks such as "**must**" can help ChatGPT focus on the essential parts of a prompt. Steps 7 and 8 describe how

CHAPTER 9   BUILDING A LANGUAGE LEARNING APP

many questions there are in the quiz and how to examine the results, comparing the users answers with the quiz questions in a case-insensitive comparison. For incorrectly answered questions, the mnemonic is displayed. Finally, in step 9, we specify that CSS be added to make the UI look modern and to output all the code for the page as a single file.

Once the code is generated, copy it and paste it into a new file "src/pages/spelling-quiz.js". Then, start the web app if it isn't already running, and in your browser, navigate to http://localhost:3000/spelling-quiz. You should have a functioning interface to play the quiz, an example of which is shown in Figure 9-3. Your UI may look different as ChatGPT does not generate the same code each time. If your UI throws errors or does not behave as expected, then in ChatGPT, start a new chat, paste the prompt, and regenerate the page again. There are some common issues that ChatGPT doesn't get right with the page:

1. When entering text in the text box the images begin to change and you can't navigate "Next."

2. The layout of the UI is messy with the buttons and text boxes unaligned.

3. When reaching the end of the quiz, an error is thrown rather than going to the summary page.

CHAPTER 9   BUILDING A LANGUAGE LEARNING APP

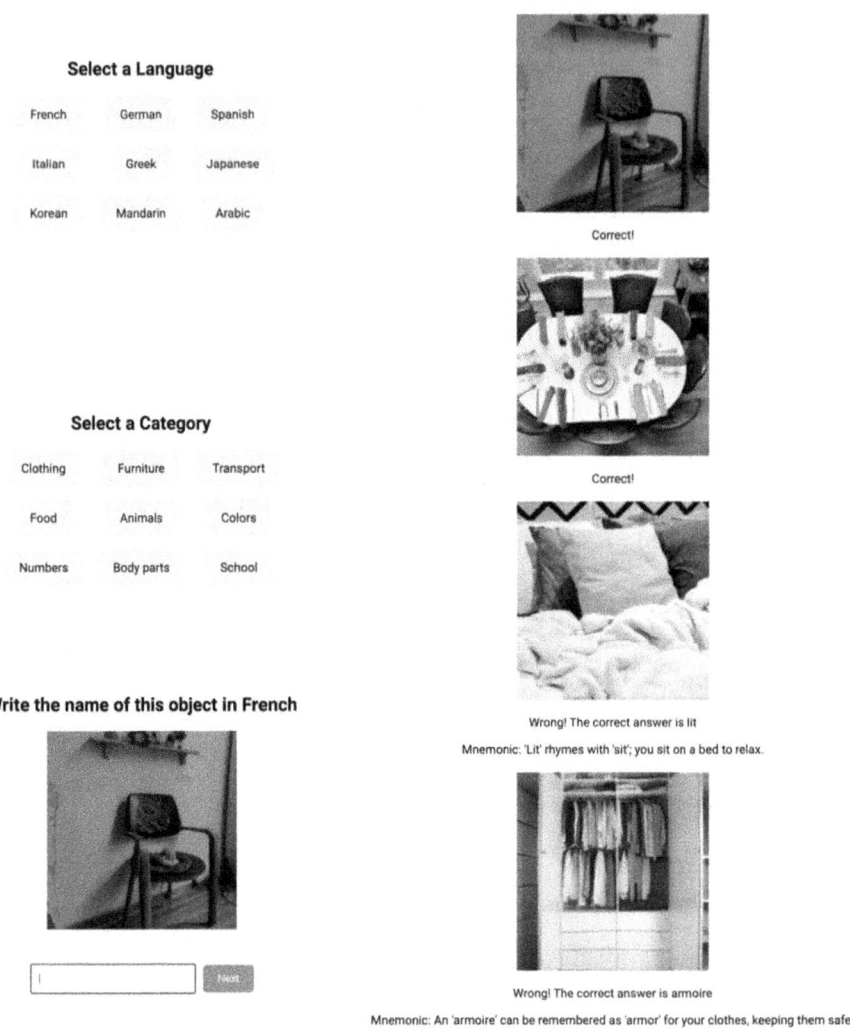

Figure 9-3. *Four screens showing playing a quiz in the spelling learning page*

CHAPTER 9   BUILDING A LANGUAGE LEARNING APP

Listing 9-11. Prompt for ChatGPT to generate the home page

I'm writing a web page in React.js with Next.js using the pages router. I'm creating a homepage that contains two circular tiles centered both vertically and horizontally on the middle of the page and spaced a bit apart. The border of the tiles is medium thick, one is blue and the other is red. When hovering over these tiles there is a shadow effect that makes the tiles lift off the page. The text inside the first tile is "Translating Quiz" and the text inside the other text tile is "Spelling Quiz". When clicking on the first tile the page navigates to the url '/translating-quiz' and when clicking on the second tile the page navigates to '/spelling-quiz'. Add some css using the styled-jsx tag to make the page look modern. Output all the code as a single file.

The prompt in Listing 9-11 instructs ChatGPT to create a page with two circular buttons. When clicked, these buttons should navigate to the translating quiz and the spelling quiz. The code should be generated in a single file. If not, send a follow-up prompt to the same chat to put the code into a single file. Once the code is generated, copy it and paste it into a new file named "src/pages/index.js". Then, run your application and navigate in your browser to http://localhost:3000/. An example home page is shown in Figure 9-4.

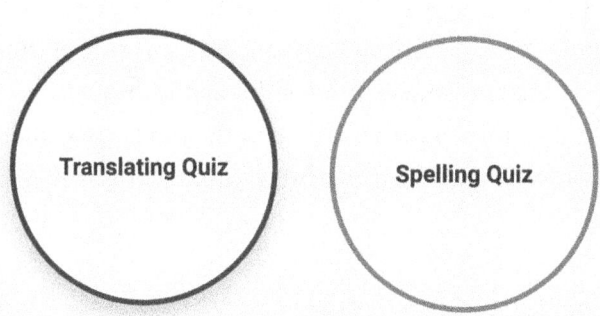

Figure 9-4. *The home page with two tiles to navigate between the translating quiz and the spelling quiz*

This completes our language learning app. To improve the app further, consider making the following enhancements:

- Add titles and navigation buttons to the translating quiz and the spelling quiz pages.

- Generate some images with DALL-E to use as backgrounds or icons.

- Add additional types of quiz, for example, presenting a word in the chosen language and the user selects an image from a series of four choices.

9.6 Summary

In this chapter, we built a language learning app with Next.js that uses the Chat API to generate quizzes to help learn new vocabulary. We learned how to use JSON schemas to get the Chat API to return quizzes in a format that can be processed by our app. We also learned how to build an interactive UI with ChatGPT that allows the user to answer the quiz questions, grade the responses, and display a summary at the end.

In the next chapter, we will build a blog with Next.js that has a built-in chat interface customized with the data in the blog posts, allowing users to ask questions and chat about the contents of the blog.

CHAPTER 10

Building a Blog with a Custom Chatbot

10.1 Introduction

One of the most useful features of chatbots like ChatGPT is the ability to ask questions and receive answers in natural language, making it faster and more straightforward to receive information than traditional search engines. While ChatGPT has been trained on a vast amount of data, it may encounter gaps in its knowledge if asked about information not included in its training set. In such cases, it may either admit its ignorance or fabricate an answer. To use ChatGPT with your own data, we must give it access to that information. In this chapter, we will explore how to do this by building a custom chatbot for a personal blog, allowing users to ask questions about the blog's content and receive answers in natural language.

We will build this project throughout the chapter step by step. However, if you wish to view or refer to the completed projects, the source code for this book is available on GitHub via the book's product page, located at www.apress.com/9798868808845.

10.2 Setting Up the Project

Before setting up the project ensure you have Node.js LTS installed. Refer to Chapter 5, Section 5.2, for instructions on how to do this.

To create the project, open a terminal and run the following command:

```
> npx create-next-app@latest interactive-blog
```

You will be prompted with the following questions on how to configure the project. To match the example in this book, answer the questions the same way. If you configure the project differently, you may need to modify the code examples to be compatible:

1. Would you like to use Typescript: **No**/Yes
2. Would you like to use ESLint: **No**/Yes
3. Would you like to use Tailwind CSS: **No**/Yes
4. Would you like to use "src/" directory: No/**Yes**
5. Would you like to use App Router: **No**/Yes
6. Would you like to customize the default import alias: **No**/Yes

After completing these commands, the project will be created in a folder called *interactive-blog*.

Next, in your terminal, change to the project folder by running:

```
> cd interactive-blog
```

and then install the OpenAI library which we will use to communicate with the OpenAI APIs:

```
> npm install openai
```

Finally, delete the template code that we don't need so that it doesn't interfere with our project:

1. First, **delete** the following files:
   - src/styles/globals.css
   - src/styles/Home.module.css
   - src/pages/api/hello.js
   - public/next.svg
   - public/vercel.svg

2. Then, open `src/pages/index.js` and delete all the content so it is a blank file.

3. Finally, open `src/pages/_app.js` and **delete** the first line: `import "@/styles/globals.css";`.

10.2.1 Configuring an OpenAI API Key

To integrate chat functionality into our project, we need to configure our app to use the OpenAI APIs. In Chapter 6, we set up an OpenAI account, created a project, and then generated an API key. If you don't have an API key, follow the steps in Chapter 6 to obtain one and copy it. Then in the project, create a new file called `.env` in the root directory of the project (Figure 10-1) and write the following:

`OPENAI_API_KEY=sk-xxx`

Replacing "sk-xxx" with your generated OpenAI API key.

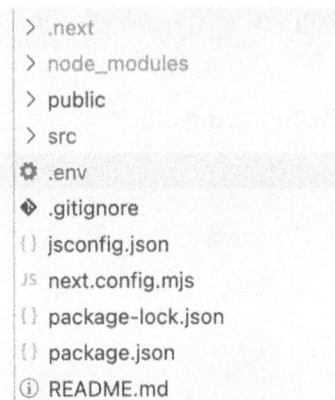

Figure 10-1. Creating the .env file for the OpenAI API key

To protect your API key, you should not commit the `.env` file to source control. If you are using git, add `.env` to your `.gitignore` file located in the *interactive-blog* folder.

This completes the setup of our project.

10.3 Creating a Basic Blog

To get started, we will create a basic blog in Next.js. Initially, we will build it without any CSS styles, and later, we will use ChatGPT to customize the appearance. The site will have a "posts" folder containing text files with the blog posts. The home page will display a list of the blog posts, and selecting one will navigate to a dedicated page to read it. To populate our site with content, we will generate some blog posts with ChatGPT.

10.3.1 Creating the Blog Skeleton

First, let's develop the code that reads the blog text files. Create the file `interactive-blog/lib/post.js`, and enter the contents from Listing 10-1.

Listing 10-1. Code for src/lib/posts.js

```
import fs from 'fs';
import path from 'path';
const postsDirectory = path.join(process.cwd(), 'posts');
export function getAllPostIds() {
    const fileNames = fs.readdirSync(postsDirectory);
    return fileNames.map(fileName => {
        return {
            params: {
                id: fileName.replace(/\.txt$/, '')
            }
        };
    });
}

export function getPostData(id) {
    const fullPath = path.join(postsDirectory, `${id}.txt`);
    const fileContents = fs.readFileSync(fullPath, 'utf8');
    // Split the file contents by line breaks
    const lines = fileContents.split('\n');
    // The first line is the title, the rest is the content
    const title = lines[0];
    const content = lines.slice(1).join('\n').trim();
    return {
        id,
        title,
        content
    };
}
```

This code reads the list of text files in the posts folder and uses the first line of each file as the title of the post.

CHAPTER 10   BUILDING A BLOG WITH A CUSTOM CHATBOT

Next, we will create the page for reading an individual blog post. Create the file src/pages/posts/[id].js, and enter the code displayed in Listing 10-2. Note that the file is called [id].js with the square brackets, and this notation means that "id" is a parameter for the page that, in this scenario, is used to identify the blog post to display.

Listing 10-2. Code for src/pages/posts/[id].js

```
import { getAllPostIds, getPostData } from '../../lib/posts';
export async function getStaticProps({ params }) {
    const postData = getPostData(params.id);
    return {
        props: {
            postData
        }
    };
}
export async function getStaticPaths() {
    const paths = getAllPostIds();
    return {
        paths,
        fallback: false
    };
}
export default function Post({ postData }) {
    return (
        <div>
            <h1>{postData.title}</h1>
            <p>{postData.content}</p>
        </div>
    );
}
```

CHAPTER 10 BUILDING A BLOG WITH A CUSTOM CHATBOT

This code renders a simple page displaying the blog post title, taken to be the first line of the text file containing the post and the content of the post displayed below it.

Finally, we will create the home page to display a list of blog posts as links which when clicked lead to the post page for reading. In src/pages/index.js, enter the code from Listing 10-3.

Listing 10-3. Code for src/pages/index.js

```
import Link from 'next/link';
import { getAllPostIds, getPostData } from '../lib/posts';
export async function getStaticProps() {
    const allPosts = getAllPostIds().map(({ params }) => {
        const postData = getPostData(params.id);
        return postData;
    });
    return {
        props: {
            allPosts
        }
    };
}
export default function Home({ allPosts }) {
    return (
        <div>
            <h1>My Blog</h1>
            <ul>
                {allPosts.map(({ id, title }) => (
                    <li key={id}>
                        <Link href={`/posts/${id}`}>
                            {title}
                        </Link>
```

```
                </li>
            ))}
        </ul>
    </div>
  );
}
```

This code retrieves a list of all the files in the *posts* folder and displays a list of links that each navigate to the post page for the selected blog post.

10.3.2 Adding Content

Now, we need to populate our website with content. If you have your own blog posts that you would like to use for the project, then feel free to use them. Otherwise, we will use ChatGPT to generate some. Since we want to build a chatbot to ask questions about the content, it would work best to have blog posts with unique information so we can prove that our custom chatbot is using their contents.

First, create the folder `src/posts`; then, from Listing 10-4, run the two example prompts in separate chats in ChatGPT to generate two blog posts with unique information. Place the generated blog posts in separate files called `post1.txt` and `post2.txt` inside the `src/posts` folder. The prompts for these blog posts include some unique details that will allow us to ask specific questions to our chatbot.

Listing 10-4. Two prompts for generating sample blog posts

```
Write for me a short blog post written by a fictional person
called Ani Abovyan. In this blog post Ani describes her hiking
trip to ascend Ararat, which she completes with her best
friend Tatev over four days. On the first day she has a great
hike with the sun beaming down and beautiful scenery. But at
the first base camp, she realises she forgot to bring her
```

If the issues are UI related, for example, the controls are not aligned properly, then the best way to fix it is to enter a follow-up prompt to ChatGPT describing the problem with the layout and asking it to fix it. If the issue is due to throwing an error, then the best remedy is to regenerate the whole page again in a new chat.

Try playing a few quizzes, and see what parts of the application work well and which require improvement. Using the techniques from Chapter 5, try improving the appearance and adding new features to the app, for example, you can ask ChatGPT to:

- Adjust the CSS to a color scheme, fonts, and layout to your preferences.
- Add animations when you transition between questions.
- Keep a record of the words answered correctly, and don't include them the next time you run that quiz.

This completes the spelling learning page. We've created two pages with different quizzes for learning vocabulary, but our app is missing a home page to navigate to them. We will create this in the next section.

9.5 Creating a Home Page

We've created two pages in our vocabulary learning app, one for generating multiple-choice questions to practice translations and another to practice spellings and remembering words. However, there is no way to navigate to them other than by typing their URLs in the address bar. In this section, we will create a home page consisting of two tiles to navigate to the two pages.

To create the page, open ChatGPT and create a new chat. Then, paste in the prompt in Listing 9-11 and run it.

toothbrush. Fortunately her friend Tatev lends her hers. On the second day they reach the summit. It's cold at the top with a lot of snow, but the visibility is perfect. They take a lot of selfies at the summit and then perform the descent. Tatev loses one of her crampons as they descend, but it causes no issues. On the third day they complete the descent and are proud of their achievement. Write the post in an informal style. The first line should be the post title.
Write for me a short blog post written by a fictional person called Ani Abovyan. In this blog post Ani describes her trip to New York in Autumn where she is staying with her friend Elya who lives in Brooklyn for two weeks. It's the first time Ani has been to the USA and she is very excited. During her time in New York, she visits the zoo in central park and is amazed by the sea lions. She visited the Statue of Liberty but the weather was cloudy and rainy and the visibility wasn't so good. She also goes on a shopping trip to Macy's where she buys a new dress. She has a great time overall and wants to go back again in the future. Write the post in an informal style. The first line should be the post title.

You can add additional blog posts, either existing or generated ones, until you have a posts folder with several examples.

To view the blog, open a terminal in the *interactive-blog* and start the website by running:

```
> npm run dev
```

Then, navigate to http://localhost:3000 and check that you can open and view the blog posts (see Figure 10-2).

CHAPTER 10   BUILDING A BLOG WITH A CUSTOM CHATBOT

Figure 10-2. Left: the blog home page with a list of posts. Right: viewing a blog post

10.3.3 Adding Styles

Our blog currently looks bland as there aren't any styles. To improve its appearance and make it look modern, we will add some CSS styles using ChatGPT.

Open ChatGPT and create a new chat. Select all the code in `src/pages/index.js` and copy it. Then, enter and run the prompt in Listing 10-5, pasting the code below the prompt. Feel free to modify the prompt to specify the colors, background, font, layout, and other styles as you desire.

Listing 10-5. Prompt to add CSS to style the blog

```
Modify this page from a Next.js app with some CSS styles using
styled-jsx to make it look modern using a light colour theme
based and a modern font. Make sure not to place a tags in the
Link component using the latest recommendations from Next.js.
Output the code as a single file.
<paste code here>
```

Copy the code you receive and paste it into `src/pages/index.js`, overwriting the existing contents.

Next, open `src/pages/posts/[id].js`, select all the code, and copy it. To apply the same styles as was generated for the home page, use the same chat in ChatGPT to enter and run the following prompt, pasting in your code below it:

CHAPTER 10   BUILDING A BLOG WITH A CUSTOM CHATBOT

Now apply the same styles to this page:
<paste code here>

Copy the generated code and replace the contents of `src/pages/posts/[id].js`. To view the changes, run the website and navigate to `http://localhost:3000` where you should see the new styles have been applied. An example is shown in Figure 10-3.

Figure 10-3. Blog with CSS styles applied

This completes the creation of our basic blog. In the next section, we will begin creating a chatbot that will allow visitors to the blog to ask questions and interact with the content.

10.4 Creating an Assistant

Creating a chatbot with the sophistication of one like ChatGPT that also has knowledge of custom data is a frequently desired capability. To address this need, OpenAI released a tool called *Assistants*, which allows you to create customized versions of the GPT models that behave in specific ways and have access to custom data. In this section, we will first provide an overview of how Assistants work, before moving on the process of creating one using our generated blog posts.

10.4.1 Fine-Tuning and RAG

There are two techniques to provide an LLM like GPT access to custom data: *fine-tuning* and *Retrieval Augmented Generation* (RAG). Large language models such as GPTs are trained on an extensive corpus of text from sources like the Internet and books, during which they memorize a lot of information. *Fine-tuning* is the process of training an LLM further on custom data, enabling it to absorb the new content. OpenAI provides a fine-tuning service with their GPT models.[1] The advantage of fine-tuning is that less information needs to be provided within prompts to explain the format of the data or its contents, as the model will have already assimilated this information. Since the costs of using the Chat API are calculated by the number of tokens (see Chapter 6, Section 6.3), this can reduce the cost significantly.

However, there are drawbacks to fine-tuning. Training LLMs is a time-consuming and expensive process, making it impractical for data that changes frequently. Furthermore, there is no guarantee that the LLM will have internalized all the information in the custom dataset, and it is not easy to verify, making it unsuitable when the accuracy of information is important. Fine-tuning is most effective when the requirement is to alter the behavior of an LLM – changing how it responds to certain prompts – rather than learning the contents of a dataset. Typically, the training data for fine-tuning consists of many example prompts paired with the desired responses, allowing the LLM to learn behavioral patterns rather than memorizing specific details.

Another method to provide custom data to a model is by including information along with the prompt. By adding custom data as *context,* an LLM can utilize this information when generating a response. However, LLMs are constrained by a limited *context length,* restricting the amount of data that can be inserted with the prompt. To overcome this, we can use

---

[1] https://platform.openai.com/docs/guides/fine-tuning

the prompt to identify and extract the parts of the custom dataset that are most relevant, incorporating as much as possible into the context. This technique is called *Retrieval Augmented Generation* (RAG). *Retrieval* is the process of selecting the relevant parts of a dataset based on a query, while *Augmented Generation* is the process of adding this selected data to the context, providing the model with the necessary information to generate an informed response. See Figure 10-4 for an illustration of this process.

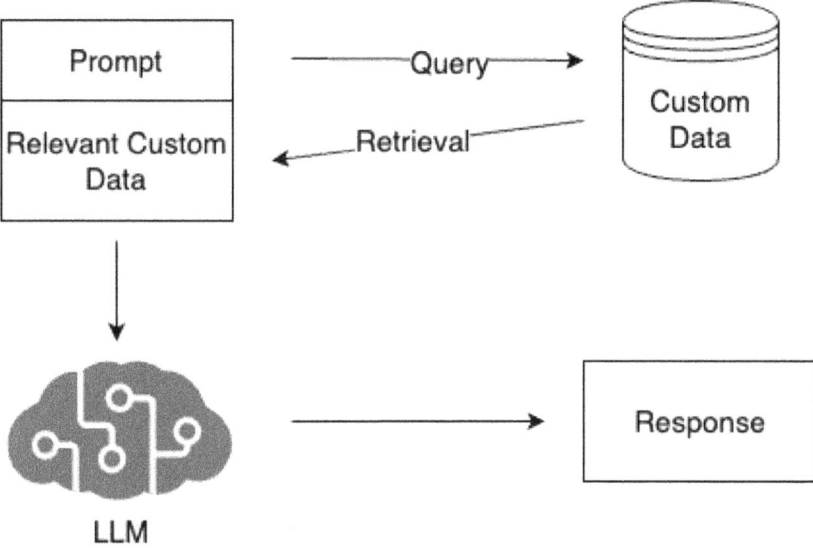

Figure 10-4. Overview of how Retrieval Augmented Generation (RAG) works

The process of querying custom data involves several key steps. Let's suppose our custom data consists of plain text documents, such as blog posts. The first step is to convert these blog posts from text to a numerical format that captures the information contained within them. This process is called creating an *embedding*. Each blog post, or chunks of them if the posts are large, are transformed into numerical vectors (a one-dimensional array of numbers). These vectors, called *embeddings*, are placed in a vector store – a type of database for efficiently storing and retrieving vectors.

To perform RAG, the user's prompt is also converted into an embedding, creating a vector that captures the essential information in the prompt. To find relevant blog posts, the prompt embedding is compared with the embeddings of the posts. This comparison is based on a measure known as cosine similarity – if the vectors are "close" to each other, it suggests that the corresponding post is relevant to the prompt. The most relevant posts are then selected and added along with the prompt, becoming part of the context the model uses to generate its response.

The advantages of RAG are that it scales well with large quantities of custom data, as calculating embeddings and comparing them can be performed efficiently. Additionally, it doesn't require modifying the LLM, making it especially useful in situations where data is frequently updated. As the context length of LLMs continues to grow, the effectiveness of RAG improves as well, allowing for more relevant data to be incorporated into the context.

RAG has proven so effective that OpenAI has built this functionality into their *Assistants* tool, simplifying the process of handling custom data and enabling the creation of custom GPTs that perform RAG.

10.4.2 Building and Testing an Assistant

To create an assistant, log in to the ChatGPT Platform (see Chapter 6, Section 6.4, for details on how to set it up). Once logged in, click "Playground" in the menu in the top right and then "Assistants" in the menu on the left-hand side. This will open the Assistants Playground as shown in Figure 10-5.

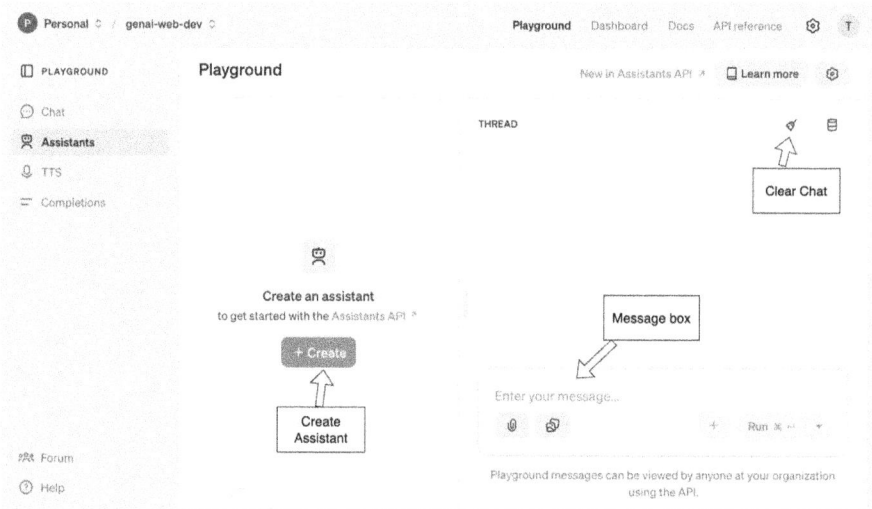

Figure 10-5. *The Assistants Playground in the OpenAI platform*

To create an assistant, click the green "Create" button. Once the assistant is created, the playground updates to show the assistant and its configuration options as shown in Figure 10-6.

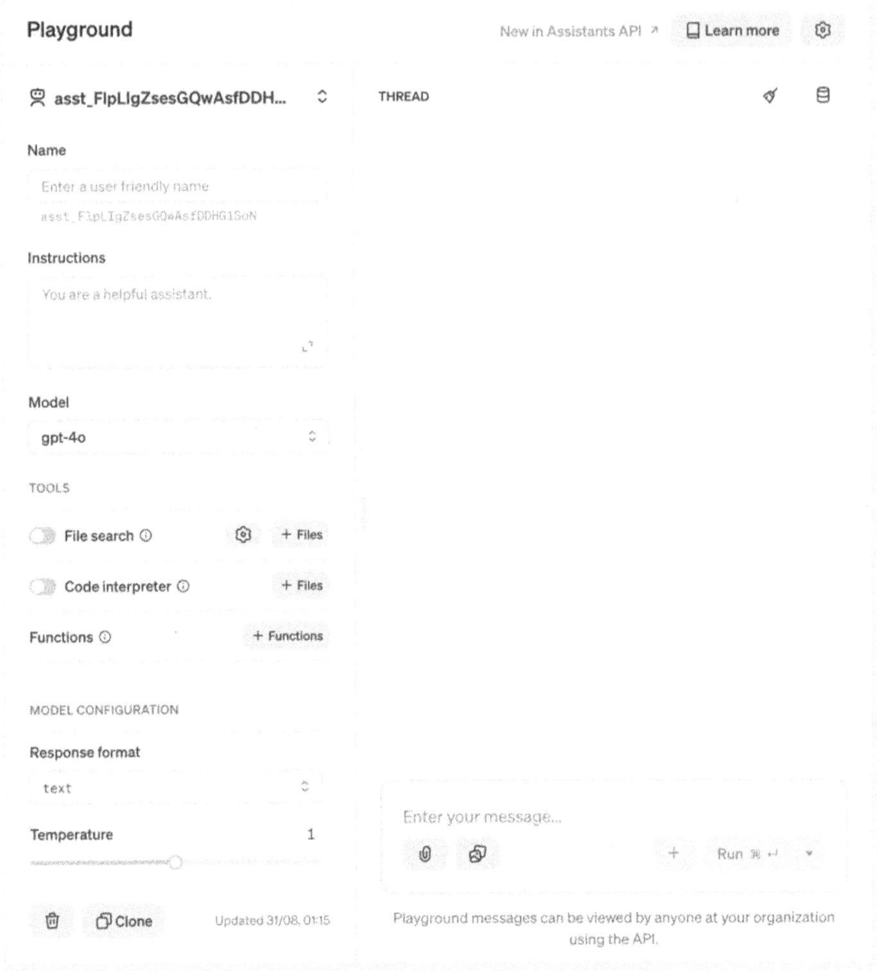

CHAPTER 10 BUILDING A BLOG WITH A CUSTOM CHATBOT

Figure 10-6. Assistant with configuration options

In the *name* field, enter a friendly name such as "Blog Assistant." Immediately below the name field is the unique ID of the assistant beginning with "*asst_*". We will use this ID later when calling the assistant via the API. The *Instructions* field contains the *system prompt* (see Chapter 3, Section 3.4.2) that describes how the assistant will respond. Enter the instruction "You are a friendly assistant for a blog written by Ani.

Respond in an informal style." If you used a different set of blog posts, then change the name Ani to the correct author and adjust the prompt as appropriate. In the *model* field, select "gpt-4o-mini," which will perform well for our chatbot while being cost-effective.

Next, in the *Tools* section, enable "File search" by clicking the toggle. Then, click the "+Files" button located next to it. This will open a dialog for uploading files to the assistant as shown in Figure 10-7.

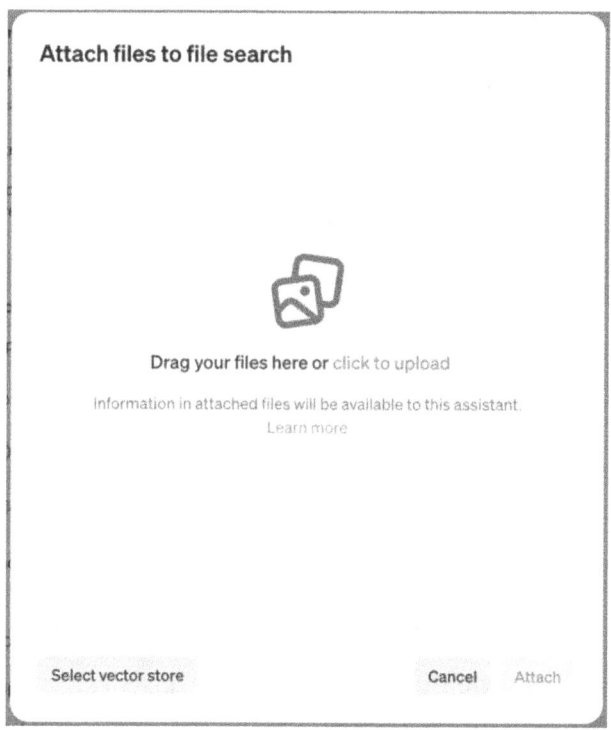

Figure 10-7. *Attaching files to the Assistant*

From the "posts" folder in the *interactive-blog* project, upload both post1.txt and post2.txt, and click "Attach." When the files are attached, they are automatically processed to create embeddings and stored in a vector store, ready to perform RAG as shown in Figure 10-8.

CHAPTER 10   BUILDING A BLOG WITH A CUSTOM CHATBOT

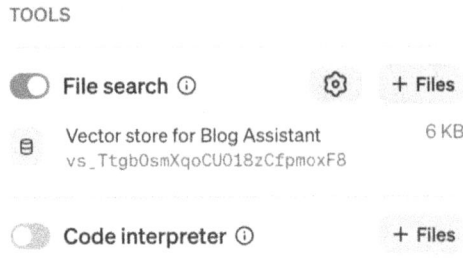

Figure 10-8. Vector store created for the blog assistant

We can now test our assistant by entering some prompts into the message box and viewing the responses. If you used the prompts from Listing 10-4 to generate the blog posts, try asking the following questions:

- Who did Ani stay with in New York?
- Which attractions did Ani see on her trip to New York?
- Does Ani like New York?
- What did Ani forget to bring when she hiked Ararat?
- How many days did it take Ani to hike Ararat?

You should see that the assistant correctly answers the questions having extracted the relevant information from the blog posts. See Listing 10-6 for an example interaction.

Listing 10-6. Example interaction with the assistant showing it correctly retrieves information

User
Who did Ani stay with in New York?
Blog Assistant
Ani stayed with her amazing friend Elya, who lives in Brooklyn during her trip to New York City. Sounds like they had an awesome time exploring the city together!

214

User

Which attractions did Ani see on her trip to New York?

Blog Assistant

During Ani's trip to New York, she checked out some pretty cool attractions! Here's a quick rundown:

1. Central Park Zoo - Ani was totally enchanted by the sea lions there. She could have watched them all day as they swam and played around.

2. Statue of Liberty - She took a ferry ride to see Lady Liberty, even though it was a cloudy day. The experience was still magical for her as she reflected on what the statue means to many who've arrived in America.

3. Macy's - Ani called it a "shopper's paradise" and treated herself to a gorgeous burgundy dress, perfect for the autumn vibe she was loving.

Sounds like she had an incredible time soaking up the NYC energy! 🗽✨.

User

What did Ani forget to bring when she hiked Ararat?

Blog Assistant

When Ani hiked Ararat, she forgot to bring her toothbrush! 😅 But no worries, her friend Tatev came to the rescue and let her borrow hers. Crisis averted, and they went on to have an amazing adventure together!

We have now built an assistant for our blog. Next, we will create a chat page for the blog where anyone can interact with the assistant using the Chat API.

10.5 Adding a Chat Interface

In this section, we will create a chat page for the blog, containing a chat interface where the user can type questions about the blog's content and receive answers from the assistant. We will begin by developing the backend code that calls the assistant we created via the Chat API and then build the user interface to perform the interactions.

10.5.1 Building the Backend

Interactions with assistants differ from the way we've previously used the Chat API. Messages sent to an assistant are part of an ongoing thread rather than standalone. When the user initiates a chat, we must first create a thread to which all subsequent messages will be added. Additionally, we will demonstrate another useful feature of the Chat API by streaming the responses back to the UI as they are generated, in the same way messages are output incrementally when prompting ChatGPT. The backend will contain two functions: one for creating threads and another for generating responses to the latest message within the thread using the assistant.

When communicating with the assistant via the API, we need to provide the assistant's ID so that the correct one is used. You can find the ID in the Assistants Playground, just below the name textbox as shown in Figure 10-9. Copy this ID, and in `interactive-blog/.env`, add the following line below the OPENAI_KEY:

```
ASSISTANT_ID=<paste your assistant id>
```

We are now ready to implement the backend functions.

Playground

🧑 Blog Assistant

Name

Blog Assistant

asst_FlpLIgZsesGQwAsfDDHG1SoN

Instructions

Figure 10-9. *Copying the assistant ID from the Assistants Playground*

Since we will use the OpenAI client in more than one place, let's create a function that instantiates it once. Create the file `src/lib/openai.js` and insert the code in Listing 10-7.

Listing 10-7. Code for "src/lib/openai.js"

```
import OpenAI from "openai";
// Initialise the OpenAI library to communicate with the OpenAI APIs
export const openai = new OpenAI();
```

Next, we'll write the function that creates a new thread when the chat begins. Create the file `src/pages/api/thread.js`, and enter the code in Listing 10-8.

Listing 10-8. Code for `src/pages/api/thread.js`

```
import { openai } from "@/lib/openai";
export default async function handler(req, res) {
    try {
        const thread = await openai.beta.threads.create();
```

CHAPTER 10   BUILDING A BLOG WITH A CUSTOM CHATBOT

```
        // Send the result to display in the UI
        res.status(200).json({ threadId: thread.id });
    } catch (error) {
        // Return an error message if the request failed
        res.status(500).json({ error: 'Failed to create
        thread' });
    }
}
```

The Assistants feature in OpenAI is, as of August 2024, still classified as *beta*, which is why the function is found in the "openai.beta" namespace. In future releases, these functions may be moved. Refer to the documentation for the latest syntax.[2]

Next, let's add a second function to generate responses to messages. We will build this function in stages. First, create the file src/pages/api/message.js and enter the code in Listing 10-9.

Listing 10-9. Initial code for "src/pages/api/message.js"

```
import { openai } from "@/lib/openai";
// Get the assistant ID from the .env file
const assistant_id = process.env.ASSISTANT_ID;
export default async function handler(req, res) {
    try {
        // Get the thread ID and message text
        const { threadId, message } = req.body;
        // ... to be implemented ...
    } catch (error) {
```

---

[2] https://platform.openai.com/docs/assistants/quickstart

```
  // Return an error message if the request failed
  res.status(500).json({ error: 'Failed to generate
  response' });
  }
}
```

The first few lines of the code retrieve the OpenAI client we instantiated in openai.js and the assistant ID we added to the .env file. The handler function then obtains the threadId and message received from the UI, all within a try-catch block to handle any potential errors.

We will return the response from the assistant as a stream so that the text appears incrementally in the UI, similar to ChatGPT. To achieve this, we need to configure the response headers that tell the web browser that data will be delivered in chunks. Insert the following code below the line that obtains the *threadId* and *message* (Listing 10-10).

Listing 10-10. Setting the response headers to enable streaming

```
// Set response headers to stream the text from the Chat API
res.setHeader('Content-Type', 'text/plain; charset=utf-8');
res.setHeader('Cache-Control', 'no-cache, no-transform');
res.setHeader('Connection', 'keep-alive');
res.setHeader('Transfer-Encoding', 'chunked');
```

With the response headers set, we can send the message to the assistant and stream the response back to the UI (Listing 10-11).

Listing 10-11. Sending and streaming the response back

```
  // Add the new message to the thread
await openai.beta.threads.messages.create(threadId, {
    role: "user",
    content: message,
    });
```

CHAPTER 10   BUILDING A BLOG WITH A CUSTOM CHATBOT

```
// Generate the response to the message and stream it to the UI
await openai.beta.threads.runs.stream(threadId, {
assistant_id })
    .on('textDelta', (textDelta) => {
        res.write(removeCitations(textDelta.value));
        res.flush();
    })
    .on('end', () => {
        // Close the stream when the response has finished
        generating
        if (!res.writableEnded) {
            res.end();
        }
    });
```

When the assistant generates a response, it also inserts citations that indicate which parts of the custom data were used. In the output, these appear as numbers between the bracket characters " 【 " and " 】 ". To avoid outputting these, we will amend the code to remove them. Add the following code above the *handler* function:

```
function removeCitations(input) {
    return input.replace(/ 【[^】]*】 /g, '');
}
```

Then, modify the line that streams the *textDelta*s to:

```
.on('textDelta', (textDelta) => res.write(removeCitations(textDelta.value)))
```

This completes the implementation. The full code for message.js is in Listing 10-12.

Listing 10-12. Complete code for "src/pages/api/message.js"

```js
import { openai } from "@/lib/openai";
// Get the assistant ID from the .env file
const assistant_id = process.env.ASSISTANT_ID;

function removeCitations(input) {
    return input.replace(/ 【[^】]*】 /g, '');
}

export default async function handler(req, res) {
    try {
        // Get the thread ID and message text
        const { threadId, message } = req.body;

        // Set response headers to stream the text from the
            Chat API
        res.setHeader('Content-Type', 'text/plain; charset=utf-8');
        res.setHeader('Cache-Control', 'no-cache, no-transform');
        res.setHeader('Connection', 'keep-alive');
        res.setHeader('Transfer-Encoding', 'chunked');

        // Add the new message to the thread
        await openai.beta.threads.messages.create(threadId, {
            role: "user",
            content: message,
        });

        await openai.beta.threads.runs.stream(threadId, { assistant_id })
            .on('textDelta', (textDelta) => {
                res.write(removeCitations(textDelta.value));
                res.flush();
```

```
        })
        .on('end', () => {
            // Close the stream when the response has
                finished generating
            if (!res.writableEnded) {
                res.end();
            }
        });
    } catch (error) {
        // Return an error message if the request failed
        res.status(500).json({ error: 'Failed to generate
        response' });
    }
}
```

This completes the implementation of the backend code. In the next section, we will implement the UI.

10.5.2 Building the UI

To create a chat interface for the blog, we'll use ChatGPT to generate the UI code. To get started, open ChatGPT and create a new chat. This prompt works best with ChatGPT 4o, so if you have a ChatGPT Plus subscription, ensure that it's enabled. If you are using ChatGPT 4o mini, you may not get good results running the whole prompt at once. Instead, you may have more success adding the prompt a few steps at a time so that the page is built incrementally. Enter and run the prompt in Listing 10-13.

Listing 10-13. Prompt to generate the chat interface for the blog

```
I'm writing a page in React.js with Next.js. The page is a chat
interface for my blog and contains a message textbox for typing
a message and a send button next to it for sending messages.
```

1. The send button is disabled if there is no text in the message textbox. Also a message can be sent by pressing enter.
2. When a message is sent, first display the user's message in the chat so it will appear above the response. Then check if it is the first message that is being sent. If it is, then POST to the endpoint 'api/thread' using fetch which returns a "threadId" in the JSON response. Store this threadId to use when sending all messages.
3. Then POST to the endpoint 'api/message' passing the "threadId" and the "message" in the body. If the thread was just created, use the threadId returned by the API rather than the react state variable. The endpoint streams the reply to the message which we should display as it arrives. The responses will be the reply that was already received plus a bit more. Follow these steps when updating the messages that are displayed:
a) Find the last message in the chat, the one at the last index.
b) If this message is from the user then add a new message to the chat that has a response type.
c) If the message is of the response type then overwrite the content with the newly received response.
4. While the message is being sent and a response being received the send message button is disabled.
5. When the response has been received the user can then send subsequent messages and the responses for these should appear below the existing ones. The focus should be placed on the message textbox.
6. Add some CSS to make this page look modern using style-jsx. Make the chat interface have 100% height, but take into account any padding so it doesn't scroll.
Output all the code as a single file.

This is a complex prompt that describes the behavior of the UI, and we encourage you to read through it to understand how it works and how to write complex prompts.

The prompt begins by introducing the technologies in use and that the page will feature a chat interface for a blog. It then breaks down the expected behavior into numbered steps, following the sequence in which these actions occur.

- **Step 1** specifies that the send button should be disabled if the message box is empty to prevent the user sending blank messages.

- **Step 2** explains that the user's message should be added to the chat so that the response is displayed immediately below it, following the typical layout of chat applications. Additionally, upon sending the first message, a new thread should be created using the backend's *thread* function, and the thread's ID should be passed with every message when generating a response.

- **Step 3** describes how to generate a response using the *message* function we created in the backend. Since the response is being streamed back, we provide detailed instructions on how the UI should be updated as the response is received. This step-by-step explanation was necessary; otherwise, ChatGPT often produced the wrong code such as overwriting previous messages in the chat.

- **Step 4** states that the message textbox and send button should both be disabled while a response is being generated to prevent the user sending messages in between.

CHAPTER 10   BUILDING A BLOG WITH A CUSTOM CHATBOT

- **Step 5** explains that the user should be able to send subsequent messages to the chat and the UI should focus on the message box to make it easy to write a reply.
- **Step 6** describes how to customize the appearance of the UI, adding CSS to make the interface look modern and fill the height of the page. All of the code will be generated in a single file to make it easy to copy the results and test it.

Once the code is generated, copy it and paste into a new file `src/pages/chat.js`. Once complete, run your website by opening a terminal in the *interactive-blog* folder and running:

```
> npm run dev
```

In a web browser, navigate to `http://localhost:3000/chat`. You should have a chat interface where you can send and receive messages using your assistant. Try asking some questions about the content of your blog such as the ones in Section 10.4.2. An example of the chat interface is shown in Figure 10-10.

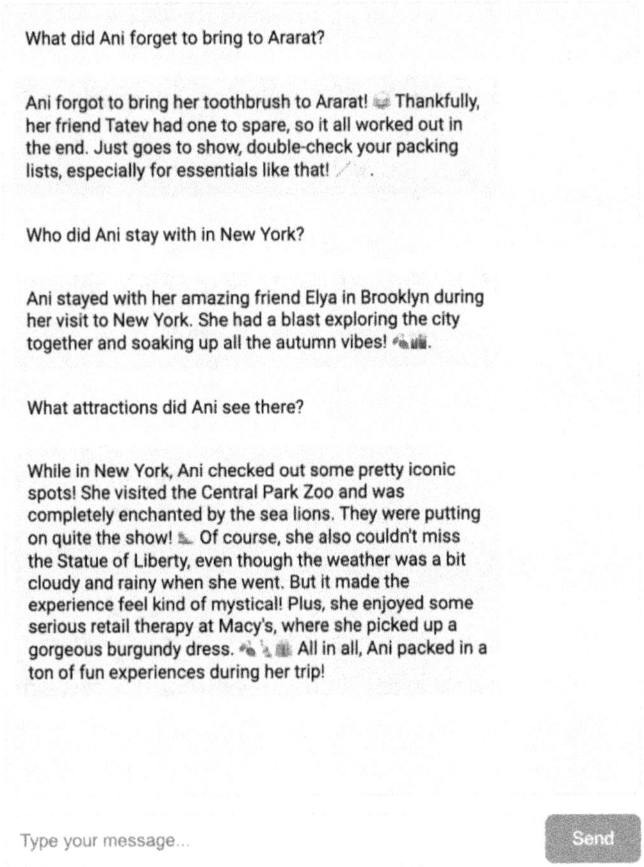

CHAPTER 10   BUILDING A BLOG WITH A CUSTOM CHATBOT

> What did Ani forget to bring to Ararat?
>
> Ani forgot to bring her toothbrush to Ararat! 😅 Thankfully, her friend Tatev had one to spare, so it all worked out in the end. Just goes to show, double-check your packing lists, especially for essentials like that! ✏️.
>
> Who did Ani stay with in New York?
>
> Ani stayed with her amazing friend Elya in Brooklyn during her visit to New York. She had a blast exploring the city together and soaking up all the autumn vibes! 🍂🗽.
>
> What attractions did Ani see there?
>
> While in New York, Ani checked out some pretty iconic spots! She visited the Central Park Zoo and was completely enchanted by the sea lions. They were putting on quite the show! 🦭 Of course, she also couldn't miss the Statue of Liberty, even though the weather was a bit cloudy and rainy when she went. But it made the experience feel kind of mystical! Plus, she enjoyed some serious retail therapy at Macy's, where she picked up a gorgeous burgundy dress. 👗🛍️. All in all, Ani packed in a ton of fun experiences during her trip!
>
> Type your message...   Send

Figure 10-10. *Example chat interface showcasing interactions with the assistant*

This completes the implementation of the chat interface. In the next section, we will finalize the project by adding a pop-up chat window into the blog's home page.

10.5.3 Adding a Pop-Up Chat

Now that we've created our chat interface, we can integrate it into our blog website via a pop-up chat window embedded into the page using an HTML iframe. We will use ChatGPT to add this feature to the home page of the blog.

Open `src/pages/index.js`, select all the code, and copy it to the clipboard. Next, open ChatGPT, start a new chat, then enter, and run the prompt in Listing 10-14, pasting in the code below the prompt.

Listing 10-14. Prompt to add the pop-up chat window to `src/pages/index.js`

```
On this Next.js page can you add a popup iframe that opens a
chat window. Add CSS to make opening the chat view smooth. The
source of the page to use for the iframe is /chat. Output the
code as a single file.
<paste code here>
```

This prompt instructs ChatGPT to add a pop-up iframe that opens a chat window, and we specify the location of the chat interface as "/chat".

Copy the generated code, and paste it into `src/pages/index.js` replacing the existing code. Then, run the website, and in your browser, navigate to the home page at `http://localhost:3000`. You should now be able to see an option to open a chat window and interact with the chat interface. An example of how this should appear is shown in Figure 10-11.

CHAPTER 10   BUILDING A BLOG WITH A CUSTOM CHATBOT

Figure 10-11. Pop-up chat interface on the blog home page

This completes the implementation of the interactive blog.

10.6 Summary

In this chapter, we built an interactive blog with a chat interface that allows users to ask questions and receive responses related to the blog posts. We learned how *fine-tuning* and *Retrieval Augmented Generation (RAG)* work and their most effective use cases. Then, we created an *assistant* in the OpenAI platform that provides gpt-4o-mini access to the blog posts, enabling it to use the information in them when generating responses.

Next, we built a chat interface for the blog, learning how to stream the outputs from the assistant so they appear in the UI incrementally as they are generated, similar to how they appear in ChatGPT. Finally, we integrated this chat interface into our blog as a pop-up chat window, enabling users of the blog to open the chat and engage in conversations about the blog's content.

In the next and final chapter, we will explore the future developments in generative AI and discuss how these advancements may impact web development in the future. Additionally, we will provide valuable resources to help you stay informed about the latest breakthroughs in generative AI.

CHAPTER 11

The Future of Generative AI

11.1 Introduction

In this chapter, we look to the future of generative AI and its implications. Since ChatGPT arrived in 2022, the pace of development in generative AI has been rapid with startups and big tech companies entering the race to create the most advanced generative AIs. In the following sections, we will explore current trends influencing the direction of innovation in generative AI and how they may develop in the future. Finally, we conclude with suggestions for further reading and resources for keeping up-to-date with the latest AI developments.

11.2 The Future of Generative AI

Since 2022, generative AI has sparked new innovations and research in both major corporations and startups. Several key debates that are taking place in the field that will determine the future direction of generative AI:

1. Open source vs. closed source?
2. Large generalist LLMs vs. small specialized LLMs?

3. Regulated vs. unregulated?
4. Transformer architecture vs. a new architecture?

In the following sections, we will explore these in greater detail.

11.2.1 Open Source vs. Closed Source

When OpenAI released GPT-1 and GPT-2, they released the source code and academic papers open source for everyone to view and use. One of the founding principles of OpenAI was to release their work openly for the benefit of everyone, hence the word "Open" in the company name. However, when ChatGPT was released based on GPT-3.5, the source code was kept closed source, and instead, access was only provided through a paid API. The decision to keep the model proprietary proved to be a commercial advantage for OpenAI, which subsequently raised $10 billion of investment from Microsoft.

The arguments presented in favor of keeping a model closed source generally fall into two categories: commercial and safety. Commercially, a closed source model is more difficult for competitors to copy and enables a flow of revenue through subscriptions to AI tools and APIs. The safety arguments typically revolve around the potential threat to humanity or national security.

In March 2023, several tech leaders, including Elon Musk, argued for a "six-month pause" in AI development citing fears about the potential negative impact of AI on humanity.[1] This was shortly followed by the resignation of Geoffrey Hinton, one of the academic leaders in AI, from his position at Google over his concerns about AI being misused for

---

[1] https://www.nytimes.com/2023/03/29/technology/ai-artificial-intelligence-musk-risks.html

CHAPTER 11   THE FUTURE OF GENERATIVE AI

disinformation and exploited by "bad actors."[2] Critics of this view argued that such calls for an "AI pause" and warnings of an "existential threat to humanity" were exaggerated, aimed at reducing the commercial lead of early AI innovators like OpenAI to slow down their development and allow competitors to catch up. OpenAI arguably played a similar tactic in March 2024 when they decided not to release Voice Engine – a voice cloning tool that could create a realistic clone with a 15-second voice sample – over fears that it would be used to create disinformation and orchestrate scams, in spite of the fact that rival companies had already released systems with similar functionality.[3]

The leading proponent of open source AI is Meta, who have released all of their Llama series of LLMs under an open source license permitting commercial use. In July 2024, Mark Zuckerberg published a letter coinciding with the release of the latest Llama 3.5 models, advocating for open source AI and pledging to keep releasing their models open source.[4] Zuckerberg's main argument is that open source development will accelerate AI progress and adoption more effectively than closed source approaches, analogous to how Linux became the dominant operating system due to its open source distribution. Companies are wary about sending their data to new and unknown AI startups for processing on LLMs. Open source AI allows them to run and fine-tune models in their own clouds or on their own hardware while keeping their data securely within their own domain.

Regarding safety, Zuckerberg suggests that open source models can be better scrutinized by academics and security experts, as there are no financial or commercial barriers preventing access. However, there is still

---

[2] https://www.theguardian.com/technology/2023/may/02/geoffrey-hinton-godfather-of-ai-quits-google-warns-dangers-of-machine-learning
[3] https://www.theguardian.com/technology/2024/mar/31/openai-deems-its-voice-cloning-tool-too-risky-for-general-release
[4] https://about.fb.com/news/2024/07/open-source-ai-is-the-path-forward/

CHAPTER 11   THE FUTURE OF GENERATIVE AI

the concern that adversaries could misuse the models to cause harm. Zuckerberg's response is that since AI models are trained on data sourced primarily from the Internet, any information an LLM reveals is information that was already publicly accessible. However, this view oversimplifies the capabilities of LLMs, particularly when it comes to disinformation and scams. LLMs have the capability to generate well-crafted fake content on a scale far beyond human capacity. Since open source models can be run without the safeguards often put in place with commercial ones, there is a significant risk that they could be used to spread and amplify fake content, potentially impacting elections, and coerce public opinion in harmful ways.[5]

Companies that advocate for open source AI are usually not doing so to give away their technology charitably. The largest open source AI companies, Meta and Mistral, only release the weights of their models and the necessary code to perform inference and fine-tuning. The data that was used to train the models is kept proprietary, making it hard for anyone to reproduce the models from scratch. The term "open weight" is increasingly being used to describe this practice, as it more accurately reflects the nature of these releases.

As of August 2024, it remains uncertain whether open source or closed source models will dominate the landscape for generative AI development and distribution. Currently, closed source models such as OpenAI's GPT-4o and Anthropic's Claude Sonnet are the most advanced LLMs available. However, Meta has been catching up, with the latest Llama 3.1 models now matching or beating the performance of rival LLMs on several benchmarks.[6] If open source LLMs catch up to the level of proprietary ones, it is likely they will become the preferred choice due to their liberal usage rights and the ability for companies to run them on their own data without needing to share it with a third party.

---

[5] https://akademie.dw.com/en/generative-ai-is-the-ultimate-disinformation-amplifier/a-68593890
[6] https://ai.meta.com/blog/meta-llama-3-1/

11.2.2 Generalist vs. Specialized LLMs

The early powerful LLMs such as GPT-3.5 and GPT-4 are significantly larger than their predecessors. One measure of the size and complexity of an LLM is the number of parameters it has. In simple terms, a parameter is a switch or gate that helps the model generate predictions. Generally, an LLM with a higher number of parameters has the potential to produce more nuanced and sophisticated outputs. For example, GPT-3 has 175 billion parameters, while GPT-4's exact number remains undisclosed by OpenAI, though it's speculated to be more than 1.7 trillion.[7]

Since the GPTs were trained on a wide and varied dataset from content on the Internet, this allows them to produce output on a variety of topics, making them generalist models. However, their considerable size makes these LLMs costly to train and maintain, rendering them impractical for companies without substantial budgets. It's important to note that the number of parameters of an LLM is not a good measure of its overall performance, as the quality of the data used for training is also a critical factor.

In April 2024, Microsoft released a family of LLMs called Phi that produce higher quality outputs for a given model size compared to rivals.[8] This reflects a growing trend toward creating smaller, specialized LLMs, designed to excel at specific tasks by being trained on high-quality datasets. Since then, numerous specialized LLMs have emerged tailored to fields including legal services,[9] drug discovery,[10] and mathematical research.[11]

---

[7] https://the-decoder.com/gpt-4-architecture-datasets-costs-and-more-leaked/
[8] https://news.microsoft.com/source/features/ai/the-phi-3-small-language-models-with-big-potential/
[9] https://www.harvey.ai/
[10] https://www.nvidia.com/en-us/clara/bionemo/
[11] https://deepmind.google/discover/blog/ai-solves-imo-problems-at-silver-medal-level/

CHAPTER 11   THE FUTURE OF GENERATIVE AI

Future generative AI systems are likely to comprise a combination of both large and small models. The generalist LLMs will continue to have the highest performance and be suited to solving complex tasks requiring expertise in several domains. In contrast, smaller LLMs, being faster and more cost-effective, will be well-suited for specialized tasks.

11.2.3 Regulated vs. Unregulated

Shortly after the release of ChatGPT, there were widespread calls for regulating AI development. The arguments presented in favor of regulation largely focused on safety concerns, from the dangers of AI-generated disinformation to the potential existential threat posed by a future "superintelligence" could harm humanity. The likelihood of such a threat remains hotly debated, with many questioning whether future AI systems could endanger humanity's existence. While AI systems are rapidly improving, the technology is still far from achieving artificial general intelligence (AGI). What many in the AI industry do agree on is the need to understand and mitigate the potential harms of current and near-future AI systems. The ethical issues outlined in Chapter 2, such as veracity, deepfakes, bias, and fairness, represent the most significant risks capable of causing harm today.

The debate on regulation also revolves around data protection and privacy. In many countries, companies must obtain consent from data owners before using their data for AI training. In Europe, where data protection laws such as GDPR are among the strictest, this prevents many companies from using data they have collected from their users for AI training. Consequently, there have been calls for the loosening of these restrictions to make it easier for companies to acquire and use data for training purposes.[12]

---

[12] https://about.fb.com/news/2024/08/why-europe-should-embrace-open-source-ai-zuckerberg-ek/

CHAPTER 11   THE FUTURE OF GENERATIVE AI

As of August 2024, progress on AI regulation has been minimal. The EU's AI Act, which came into force in August 2024, categorizes specific AI use cases into risk categories, with the aim of either banning or restricting them.[13] For example, compiling face recognition databases through untargeted scraping of internet or CCTV footage is deemed an unacceptable risk and banned, while a CV scanning system that uses AI to rank job applicants has specific legal restrictions. Although the legislation is a start, it remains weak overall, as AI use cases not explicitly mentioned in the document are by definition left unregulated.

Governments are striving to strike a delicate balance in regulating AI while aiming to avoid stifling innovation. Excessive regulation could drive AI companies to operate in countries with fewer restrictions, depriving the regulating nations of potential technological and economic benefits. On the other hand, insufficient regulation risks allowing potential harms to escalate unchecked. As legislation lags far behind the pace of technological innovation, the emergence of strict AI regulations in the near future seems unlikely. While companies and governments are still determining what constitutes acceptable AI use cases and practices, the industry is likely to remain largely unregulated.

11.2.4 Transformers vs. Another Architecture

As we discussed in Chapter 1, LLMs are built using the *transformer* architecture, developed by a team of AI engineers at Google Brain in 2017. Since then, every LLM has used this architecture, scaled up to create larger models with some adjustments and improvements. However, there is likely a limit to how far scaling the architecture will go, and researchers are already exploring the next significant breakthrough that could pave the way for more advanced AI systems.

---

[13] https://artificialintelligenceact.eu/

CHAPTER 11   THE FUTURE OF GENERATIVE AI

Yann LeCun, Chief AI Scientist at Meta, openly advised PhD students interested in building the next generation of AI systems to work on something other than LLMs.[14] A segment of the AI community shares the view that the current architecture of LLMs offers limited scope for further improvement and a new breakthrough is needed for the next wave of advancements. Meanwhile, LLMs are expected to continue improving through tweaks and enhancements, as companies find ways to improve the performance of models and integrate them into existing systems

11.3 Further Reading

Since 2022, the pace of innovation in generative AI has been unprecedented. Companies such as OpenAI have been releasing new features every few months, and startups are popping up to apply AI to numerous sectors. Staying informed about the AI industry is a challenge, as there is no single source to get news. In this section, we list some useful resources to follow that will help keep you informed about developments in generative AI:

1. **Hacker News:** YCombinator's news aggregator remains one of the best places to discover the latest releases and innovations in AI as well as the tech industry as a whole: https://news.ycombinator.com/.

2. **OpenAI Blog:** Follow OpenAI's blog to keep up-to-date with the latest releases and innovations: https://openai.com/news/.

3. **Meta AI Blog:** Follow the latest releases from Meta AI: https://ai.meta.com/blog/.

---

[14] https://x.com/ylecun/status/1793326904692428907?lang=en

4. **OneUsefulThing:** Ethan Mollick is a professor of Management at Wharton who actively writes about how to make the most of the latest generative AI tools. His blog, *OneUsefulThing*, as well as his recent book *Co-Intelligence: Living and Working with AI* are informative general guides on how to use generative AI: https://www.oneusefulthing.org/.

5. **AI Snake Oil:** Arvind Narayanan and his doctoral student Sayash Kapoor discuss through this blog, and their book with the same title, the negative and dubious sides of AI and how to identify hype from reality in the AI industry: https://www.aisnakeoil.com/.

6. **DeepLearning.ai:** Educational courses on AI by Andrew Ng, ranging from the foundations of machine learning to ChatGPT and generative AI: https://www.deeplearning.ai/.

11.4 Summary

The advent of generative AI is transforming the way web developers approach their work. Stack Overflow used to be the main resource for engineers to find solutions to programming problems. Now, generative AI tools such as ChatGPT and GitHub Copilot are being integrated into IDEs to generate and debug code and provide advice and suggestions.

Not only is AI changing the way web developers work, it is also altering the nature of projects developers are building. Intelligence is a general-purpose capability, and AI is being integrated into applications in almost every sector. Given that large generative AI models require substantial computing power, they will be primarily hosted in the cloud and accessed

CHAPTER 11 THE FUTURE OF GENERATIVE AI

via APIs. This dependency on Internet connectivity, together with the push to integrate AI everywhere, means that web developers – whether backend or frontend engineers – will almost inevitably work with AI during their careers.

In this book, we have explored the world of generative AI for web development, beginning with the fundamentals of how large language models like GPT-4 and diffusion models like DALL-E work. We explored how to use ChatGPT to generate code for web applications and how to integrate with the OpenAI APIs to bring AI functionality to web apps. We then built three applications step by step, demonstrating how to use ChatGPT to generate code by writing detailed prompts and how to use the Chat API, Image API, and Assistants to develop novel features such as story generation, quiz generation for language learning, and chat interfaces for custom data.

Your journey with generative AI has only just begun. It is a rapidly evolving field, and every year is likely to bring enhancements and new innovations that make this one of the most exciting areas of technology to work in.

Index

A

Absurd wokeness, 22
Advanced generative AIs, 231
Adversarial attacks, 4
AGI, *see* Artificial general intelligence (AGI)
AI, *see* Artificial intelligence (AI)
AI community, 238
AI detection tool, 20
AI development, 24, 46, 231, 232, 234, 236
AI functionality, 116, 240
AI pause, 233
AI regulation, 237
AI Snake Oil, 239
AI Studio, 118, 119
AlexNet, 4
Anthropic's Claude Sonnet, 234
API, *see* Application Programming Interface (API)
API endpoint, 90, 91, 109, 138
Application Programming Interface (API)
    chat and image generation, 87
    costs and expenses, 89
    OpenAI (*see* OpenAI APIs)
Armenian carpet, 74, 76
Artificial general intelligence (AGI), 9, 236
Artificial intelligence (AI), 4
    automatic crime detection, 4
    for detection and prediction, 5
    GANs, 5
    general, 9
    image-generating, 11
    LLMs, 7
    OpenAI, 7
    training, 5
    transforming, 6, 7
    web development, 12
Assistants
    attaching files, 213
    building and testing, 210–215
    definition, 207
    fine-tuning and RAG, 208–210
    Playground, 210, 211, 217
    vector store, 214
Audio API, 88
AWS, 122

B

Backend functions, 168, 182, 216
Backend's thread function, 224

INDEX

Base64, 152, 154, 187, 190
Basic blog creation
    adding content, 204, 205
    adding styles, 206, 207
    blog skeleton, 200–204
Batch API, 92
Batch pricing, 91–92
Beta, 218
Blog assistant, 212, 214, 215
Blog posts, 196, 200, 202–207, 209, 210, 213, 214, 228, 229

C

Carpets-website, 66
Chain-of-thought
    prompting, 36–38
Chat API, 88, 112, 169, 183
    generating text, 116
    pricing, 89, 90
    rate limits, 93, 94
Chatbots, 7, 10, 20, 27, 28, 124, 197–229
ChatGPT, 17, 48, 87, 136–140, 152, 162, 163, 165, 175–177, 179, 180, 187, 188, 190, 191, 193, 194
    active users, 8, 27
    capabilities, 29, 38
    commercial secrets, 24
    creativity, 33
    custom instructions, 43–46
    definitions, 31, 32
    describing, 28
    employs, 10
    fake references, 18
    features, 32
    free access, 29
    free tier, 28
    generated incorrect references, GPT-4o, 18, 19
    and GitHub Copilot, 12
    GPT-4 models, 8
    history, 29
    instructions, 36
    interface, 30
    knowledge, 23
    LLMs, 39
    logic puzzles, 17, 18
    log in, 30
    mobile app, 38
    natural language, 197
    new interaction, 33
    OpenAI, 28
    performance, 117
    Plus subscription, 31, 49
    prompting
        chains of thought, 34–36
        multimodal
            prompting, 36–38
        strategies, 35
    sign up, 29
    skeleton code, 70
    software engineering and web development, 9
    speech capabilities, 38
    success and performance, 9
    system prompt, 43–46

text generation, 9
text prediction, 39–43
tokenization, 39–43
training set, 35
truthfulness and
 correctness, 19
Upgrade plan, 29
versions, 28, 30
web apps (*see* Web apps)
ChatGPT-4o, 18, 108, 137
ChatGPT-4o mini, 28–30, 42,
 88, 90, 91, 93, 94, 137, 176,
 188, 222
ChatGPT Plus subscription, 49,
 176, 188, 222
Chat interface
 backend development, 216–222
 interactions, 226
 UI development, 222–226
Claude, 120–122, 128, 234
Closed source AI, 232
Closed source models, 232, 234
Codestral for code
 generation, 122
Confabulation, 18
Contact page, 63, 82–84
Content-generator-app, 107,
 108, 110
Context, 23, 39, 137, 208–210
Context length, 39, 40, 42, 46, 105,
 118, 208, 210
Cosine similarity, 210
Custom GPTs, 28, 210
Custom instructions, 43–46

D

DALL-E, 10, 87
 chat interface, 53
 DALL-E 3, 49–56
 describes, 47
 diffusion, 48
 edits, 56–61
 extensive dataset of images, 48
 generating images, 107
 image qualities and
  resolutions, 49
 performance, 117
 stages of generation process, 48
 style descriptions, 55
 style suggestions, 53, 54
 variations, 56–61
 version, 48, 49
 web apps (*see* Web apps)
DALL-E 2, 10, 48, 49, 88, 91,
 185, 186
DALL-E 3, 48, 49, 123
 advantages, 125
 API, 124
 artistic styles, 55
 chat interface, 50
 color schemes, 56
 generating images
  aspect ratio, 54, 55
  concepts, 54
  detailed prompt, 53
  prompts, 51–53
  simple prompt, 50, 51
  viewing options, 51, 52

INDEX

DALL-E 3 (*cont.*)
   perspectives and angles, 56
   specific descriptions, 55
Data privacy laws, 4
Data protection laws, 122, 236
Deepfakes, 17–21, 236
DeepLearning.ai, 239
Diffusion, 48, 240
Digital photography, 20

E

Embedding, 122, 209, 210, 213
Embeddings API, 88, 91, 92
.env file, 110, 112, 136, 157, 168, 199, 200, 219
Ethical issues, 236

F

Face recognition databases, 237
Fetch, 137, 138, 177, 189, 223
Fine-tuning, 43, 46, 208, 228
Fine-tuning API, 88
Future of generative AI
   generalist *vs.* specialized LLMs, 235, 236
   key debates, 231
   open source *vs.* closed source, 232–234
   regulated *vs.* unregulated, 236, 237
   transformers *vs.* another architecture, 237, 238

G

GANs, *see* Generative adversarial networks (GANs)
Gemini, 22, 118–120, 128
Gemma, 120, 128
Gemma 2, 120
Generalist models, 235
Generate images, 5, 10, 49, 56, 88, 109, 113, 114, 125–127
Generate Text, 88, 109, 111–113
Generative adversarial networks (GANs), 5
Generative AI, 133
   bias, 22–24
   chatbots, 20
   copyright, 15, 16
   DALL-E (*see* DALL-E)
   deepfakes, 17–21
   development history, 3
   fairness, 21–23
   functionality, 116
   liability, 15, 16
   and practical guidance, 3
   safety, 23, 24
   security, 23, 24
   tools, 239
   veracity, 17–21
Generative pretrained transformer (GPT), 7
   ChatGPT, 7–9 (*see also* ChatGPT)
   custom, 28
   LLM, 43

Genres, 146–148
GitHub Copilot, 12, 239
Google Cloud, 122
GPT, *see* Generative pretrained transformer (GPT)
GPT-3.5, 28, 232, 235
GPT-4, 28, 30, 36
GPT-4 mini, 28
GPT-4o, 28, 30, 36, 40, 42, 118, 119, 121, 122, 142, 170
gpt-4o-2024-08-06, 173
GPT-4o mini, 28–30, 42, 88, 90, 91, 93, 103, 111, 119, 170, 173, 185, 186, 213, 229
gpt-4o-mini-2024-07-18, 173

H

Hacker News, 238
Handler function, 112, 219, 220
Home page
    ASCII-generated layout, 69, 70
    ChatGPT, 74–76
    color scheme and styles, 72
    completed design, 77, 78
    CSS styles, 72, 73
    DALL-E, 74
    designs, 70
    generated image, Armenian carpet, 74
    HTML and CSS code, 70, 71
    minimal design, 71, 72
    modify the background images, 74
    product images, 75, 76
    product section, 76
    prompts, 71
    react-icons library, 77
    readability of text, 75
    social media, 77
    testimonial section, 76, 77
    text style, 75
    wireframe layouts, 69

I

Illustrations, 151–156
Image analysis, 36
Image APIs, 88
    pricing, 90, 91
    rate limits, 93, 94
imageb64, 187, 190
Image generation models
    DALL-E 3, 123
    Midjourney, 126–128
    Stable Diffusion, 123–125
Instructions, 212
Interactive-blog, 198, 200, 205, 213, 225
Internet connectivity, 240

J, K

JavaScript Object Notation (JSON), 137–139, 144, 166, 169, 170, 172, 173, 177, 179, 184, 186, 187, 189, 190, 195

INDEX

JSON, *see* JavaScript Object Notation (JSON)
JSON response, 223

L

Language learning app
   ChatGPT, 165
   create home page, 193–195
   setting up project
      configure OpenAI API key, 167, 168
      create project, 166
      delete template code, 167
      install libraries, 166
   vocabulary spelling quiz
      create backend function, 182–187
      DALL-E, 182
      generate-spelling-quiz.js, 183
      spelling quiz, 186
      spelling quiz questions, 184
      testing spelling knowledge, 182
      UI implementation, 187–193
   vocabulary translating quiz
      building the backend functionality, 168–175
      Chat API, 171
      generate-translate-quiz.js, 175
      generate-translating-quiz.js, 169

QuizTemplate JSON schema
   in zod, 170
   UI implementation, 175–182
La Platforme, 123
Large language models (LLMs), 7, 39, 40, 42, 43, 45, 240
Large 2 model, 122, 123
Legislation lags, 237
Literature, 149–151
LLama, 120–123, 128, 233, 234
LLMs, *see* Large language models (LLMs)

M

Magic-carpets-website, 65, 66, 71
Message function, 224
Meta AI Blog, 238
Meta's Llama models, 120
Midjourney, 10, 11, 123, 125–128
Mistral AI, 122, 123
Multimodal prompting, 36–38

N

Nemo model, 122
Next.js, 63, 64, 137
   api directory, 66
   configure, 107
   content generating app, 108
      Chat API, 111, 112
      code, 111

INDEX

code for generate-
  image.js, 113
Generate Text, 112, 113
Image API, 114
image generated using
  image API, 114, 115
OpenAI API library, 112
creation, 65–68
default template, 67, 68
delete the template code, 108
generating images using
  DALL-E, 107
generating text using Chat
  API, 107
LTS installed, 107
OpenAI API key, 110
OpenAI API Node.js library
  install, 108
pages directory, 66
project structure, 66, 67
run the command, 107
UI generation, 108–110
Node.js, 64, 65
Node.js LTS, 107, 133, 166, 198

O

OneUsefulThing, 239
OpenAI, 7, 9, 167
  AI detection tool, 20
  cautions, 16
  ChatGPT, 7–9
  DALL-E, 10
  documentation, 93
  fine-tuning, 43
  user chats, 23
OpenAI API key configuration,
  199, 200
OpenAI API library, 112, 134
OpenAI API playground
  element descriptions, 102
  model selector, 103
  overview, 102, 103
  parameters
    frequency penalty, 105
    GPT model, 104
    maximum tokens, 105
    presence penalty, 105
    temperature, 105, 106
    top P, 105
  prompt using Chat API via,
    103, 104
  text-to-speech, 102
  web-based interface, 102
OpenAI APIs, 184
  API account creation
    add credits, 97, 98
    add payment details, 96, 97
    create project, 95, 96
    log in, 95
  API key creation
    copy and securely store, 100
    go to the API keys
      page, 98, 99
    secret key, 99
  API key secure
    do not commit keys to
      git, 101

247

INDEX

OpenAI APIs (*cont.*)
    rotate keys periodically, 101
    store API keys
        securely, 101
  API playground, 102–106
  audio API, 88
  Chat API, 88
  ChatGPT, 87
  DALL-E, 87
  embeddings API, 88
  fine-tuning, 88
  image API, 88
  with Next.js, 107–115
  personal organization and
    default project, 94
  pricing
    audio, fine-tuning and
      embedding, 91
    batch, 91, 92
    Chat API, 89, 90
    image APIs, 90, 91
    pay-as-you-go with
      credits, 92
  usage limits, 92–94
"openai.beta" namespace, 218
OpenAI Blog, 238
"openai.chat.completions.create"
    function, 143
OPENAI_KEY, 216
OpenAI library, 142, 198
Open source AI
    companies, 232–234
Open source models,
    128, 233, 234

P

Pesponse_format parameter, 172
Phi, 235
Pop-up chat
  blog home page, 228
  HTML iframe, 227
  src/pages/index.js, 227
Prisma, 156
  Client, 159
  Client library, 158
  library, 135, 160
  prisma.schema, 157
Product pages, 63, 71, 78–83, 133, 165, 197

Q

QuizTemplate, 170, 171, 185

R

Rate limits, 93, 94, 185
Rate per day (RPD), 93
Rate per minute (RPM), 93
Result text, 109
Retrieval Augmented Generation (RAG), 208–210, 213, 228
Roles, 143
RPD, *see* Rate per day (RPD)
RPM, *see* Rate per minute (RPM)

S

SQLite, 156
SQLite database, 135

INDEX

src/pages/api/message.js file, 218
src/pages/index.js file, 203, 206
src/pages/posts/[id].js file, 202, 206
Stable Assistant, 124, 125
Stable Diffusion, 123–125
Stack Overflow, 239
"stories.db" database, 158
Story-generator-app, 134
Story generator UI, 137, 139, 140, 146, 149
Story/poetry generator
   add library page
      library UI, 159–161
      save the stories, 156–159
   backend creation, ChatGPT
      example, generated story, 145
      generated code, story prompt, 141
      generate story, 141–145
   create UI, 136–140
   example, generated poetry, 151
   genres, 146–148
   home page creation, 162, 163
   illustrations, 151–156
      with DALL-E, generate-story.js, 153
   literature, 146, 149–151
   setting up project
      configure OpenAI API key, 135, 136
      create project, 134
      delete template code, 135
      the OpenAI API library, 134
      Prisma library, 135
      story-generator-app, 134
Superintelligence, 236
System prompt, 43–46, 102, 172, 212

T

Temperature, 43, 46, 105, 106, 112
textDeltas, 220
Text generation models
   Claude, 120, 121
   Gemini, 118–120
   LLama, 121, 122
   Mistral AI, 122, 123
Text prediction, 39–43
Thread function, 217, 224
ThreadId and message, 219
Tiktoken, 40
Tiktokenizer, 40, 41
Tokenization, 39–43
Tokenizer, 40, 41
Tokens, 40, 41, 45, 89
Tokens per minute (TPM), 93
TPM, *see* Tokens per minute (TPM)
Transcribing audio, 36
Transformer architecture, 6, 7, 10, 212, 237

U

Unicode, 39, 41
User, 144

249

INDEX

V

Veracity of generative AI, 17–21
Visual language elements, 33
Vocabulary learning app, 193
Voice Engine, 233

W, X, Y, Z

Web apps
    built-in routing, 63
    contact page, 83, 84
    home page, 69–78
    macOS, 64
    Next.js, 63–68
    Node.js installation, 65
    product pages, 79–82
    project template
        cleaning, 68, 69
    server-side rendering, 63
    Windows, 64
Web development
    in AI, 12, 240

GPSR Compliance

The European Union's (EU) General Product Safety Regulation (GPSR) is a set of rules that requires consumer products to be safe and our obligations to ensure this.

If you have any concerns about our products, you can contact us on

ProductSafety@springernature.com

In case Publisher is established outside the EU, the EU authorized representative is:

Springer Nature Customer Service Center GmbH
Europaplatz 3
69115 Heidelberg, Germany

www.ingramcontent.com/pod-product-compliance
Lightning Source LLC
LaVergne TN
LVHW010339260326
834688LV00036B/779